Illustrated Guide
OCCULT ALPHABETS
SCRIPTS and CIPHERS
of the Western Mystical Tradition

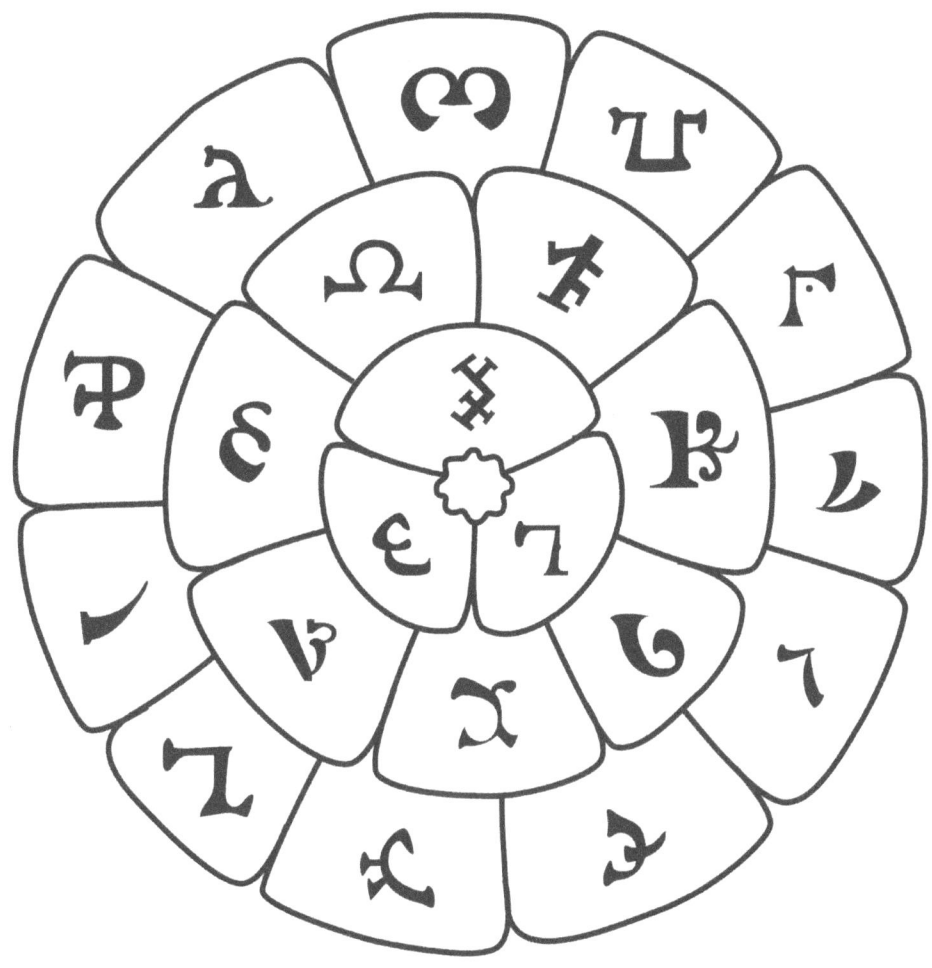

M B Jackson

GREEN MAGIC

Occult Alphabets © 2024 by Mark Jackson.
All rights reserved. No part of this book may be used or reproduced in any form without written permission of the Author, except in the case of quotations in articles and reviews.

Green Magic
Seed Factory
Aller
Langport
Somerset
TA10 0QN
England
www.greenmagicpublishing.com

Designed and typeset by Carrigboy, Wells, UK.
www.carrigboy.co.uk

ISBN 978 1 915580 20 7

GREEN MAGIC

Contents

WRITING AND THE ALPHABET

Origins of the Alphabet	6
Shamanic Symbolism	8
Schema	10
Astrograms	12
Gods of Writing	14
Scribes of the Gods	16
Numbers, Letters, Numerals	18
Ancient Writing	20
Ancient Scripts	22
Phoenician Alphabet	24
Mythological Greek Alphabet	26

OCCULT ALPHABETS

Ideograms and Mnemonics	30
Chaldean Cabala	32
Greek Cabala	34
Isosephy/Gematria	36
Correspondence	38
Jewish Cabala	40
Celestial Alphabet	42
Sephirothic Tree	44
Arabic Cabala	46
Armenian Alphabet	48
Runic Futhark	50
Rune Staves	52
Runic Oracle	54
Tree Ogham	60
Enochian Alphabet	62
Geomantic Characters	64

SCRIPTS AND CIPHERS

Hebrew Scripts	68
Syriac and Persian Scripts	70
Arabic and Ethiopian Scripts	72
Uncial Scripts	74
Roman Letters	76
Cyrillic Scripts	78
Chaldean Scripts	80
Angelic/Celestial Scripts	84
Enochian Scripts	88
Occult Scripts	90
Hermetic Scripts	92
Aleister Crowley's Scripts	94
British Neopagan Scripts	96
Aiq Bkr Cipher	98
Masonic Ciphers	100
Sigil Ciphers	102

Writing and the Alphabet

No study of occult alphabets, scripts and ciphers would be complete without a comprehensive understanding of the evolution of writing, numerals and the phonetic alphabet, the basic components of any occult alphabet.

Writing renders language visible, it is a form of human communication that employs a set of visible marks to record human speech or language. It is thought that writing was invented to store information for posterity, serving as the archival function of political, religious, scientific and literary interest. More commonly, writing is used for the mundane purposes of business accounting, personal correspondence and notes.

The history of writing is, in part, a matter of discovery and representation of the structural levels of spoken language including sentences, words, syllables and phonemes – the smallest units of speech, A, B, C, etc. It was this process that led to the creation of the phonetic alphabet.

The dictionary definition of a phonetic alphabet is – a set of symbols or letters arranged in a fixed order, used to represent the basic set of speech sounds or phonemes in a language. Phonetics is the study of writing speech signs, it takes its name from ancient Canaanite merchants called the Phoenicians, who are credited with perfecting the first one sound – one sign system of writing or alphabet.

The alphabet has been referred to as the greatest invention of mankind but mystery still surrounds its origins. These mysteries can be found in occult, mythological and academic sources that range from being a 'gift of the gods' to the earthly process of phonetic and graphic reduction of picture-word signs into an alphabet, amongst many others

Although it may originate in the shamanic symbolism of mankind's prehistory, scholars suggest that the first one sign – one system of writing originated in ancient Egypt around 1500 BCE, a result of the phonetic reduction of words into syllables and consonants speech sounds, represented by hieroglyphs. The driving force behind the invention was the growing burden of religious, administrative and economic pressures early civilizations found themselves under.

In 1050 BCE, the Phoenicians perfected the Egyptian system with influences from Crete, to create a consonant only alphabet for writing Semitic languages such as Phoenician, Hebrew and Aramaic. Phoenician merchants are known to have used the alphabet, written in a cursive, linear script or hand writing, to simplify their international trade receipts with the Egyptians, Babylonians, Assyrians and Greeks.

The Phoenician system proved so successful that it was adapted by the Hellenic Greeks around 800 BCE to write their Indo-European language, employing vowel and consonant signs to create the world's first true alphabet.

Origins of the Alphabet

There are a variety of academic theories on the origins of the letter forms of the alphabet, whereas its mythological history is still shrouded in mystery. Occultists are more certain, believing them to be a gift from God.

According to occult tradition, the original alphabet was formulated by God to create the universe through the utterance of divine language – sonic vibration. This is revealed in the Bible by the phrase "In the beginning was the Word and the Word was with God".

In science, the Word is the Big Bang. In the Vedic tradition of Hinduism, the Word is Om/AUM, the seed syllable from which all the sounds of human language are derived. In Judeo-Christian and Buddhist mysticism, the sacred sound is A or Ah or AMH.

Academic notions of the origins include the Articulatory alphabet theory, in which the letters of the alphabet are diagrammatic signs representing a picture of the positions or movements of the mouth, lips, teeth, throat and tongue, used in producing the individually distinct sounds of the alphabet.

If the alphabet can be seen as a set of diagrams of how speech sounds should be formed, then it becomes a much more useful and interesting instrument for the teaching of reading.

The characters of the Korean writing system of Han'gul and the ancient Brahmi script of the Hindu's are considered to have their graphic origins in the articulatory alphabet.

The Accidental alphabet theory suggests the alphabet was not a systematic alphabet, invented by a single tribe or civilization. It developed from a wide body of signs, mainly trademarks especially potters' marks, that were interchanged by trade and spread from land to land until a couple of dozen signs triumphed to form the alphabet.

The mythological origins of writing and the letters of the alphabet begin in man's prehistoric past with shamanic symbolism.

In many cases it is difficult or impossible to discern the basis upon which occult signs are formed. Several occult alphabets of the astro-alphabet category are considered to be derived from symbolic forms found within the construct of particular cosmograms called schema, diagrams that depict the universe. The letter forms found within them symbolize the individual cosmic forces of creation.

Similarly, astrogram is a term used to describe a diagram of a star constellation. The constellations of the zodiac are astrograms but the signs of the zodiac are glyphs. The most recent theories on the origins and development of writing lean towards the astronomical notation of the lunar zodiac or calendar, as the force that gave us the alphabet.

Early civilizations credited the invention to their Gods. Greek myth recalls that the letters of the alphabet survived the Great Flood as calculi, numbers inscribed on the knuckle bone of oxen used for calculations, as gaming dice and a divination system, in a similar manner to that of rune stones.

The notion of the alphabet originally being an alpha-numeric script is a popular theory, as certain numerals, I, V, and X, are often offered as proof of the numerical origins of letters.

The official academic explanation of the conventional origins of the letters of the alphabet is, that ancient man developed a set of picture symbols he adapted to work as phonetic place holders for the purpose of recording spoken language. This process was achieved by the phonetic and graphic reduction of word signs or pictograms into purely phonetic signs called letters.

Om / AUM   A - Alpha   Ah - Aleph   AMH - Seed Syllable Supreme
Hindu   Christian   Hebrew   Mahayana Buddhism

Seed Sounds - OM and A, Ah and Amh

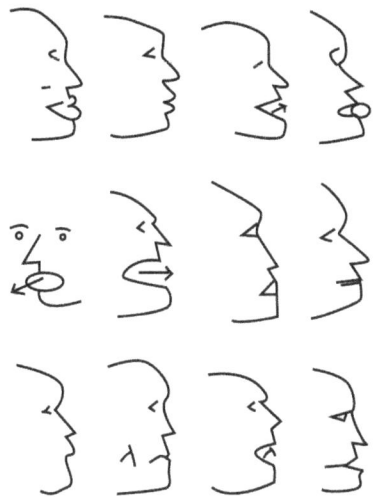 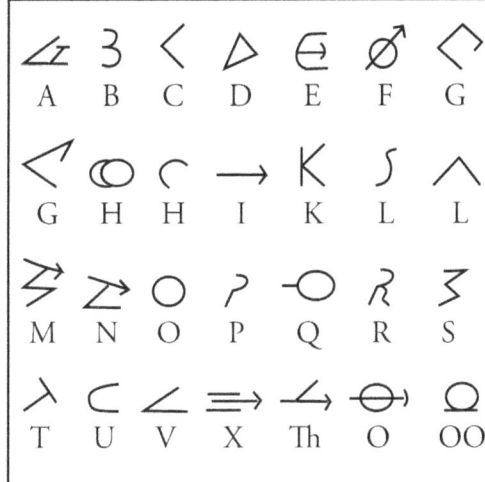

Articulatory Alphabet

Accidental Alphabet

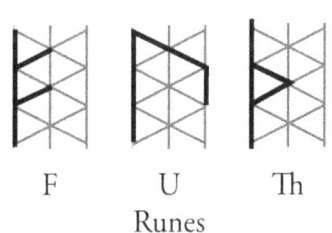  

F U Th   G B A
Runes   Hebrew

Schema / Cosmograms

 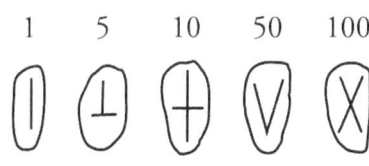

Tally numbers - Ogham script   Calculi - numerals

Alpha-numeric script

Ox / A - the graphic transition from picture sign to linear sign to letter

Shamanic Symbolism

The occult origins of the letters of the alphabet lay in the shamanic symbolism of prehistory. Symbolism is the way our ancestors took all information as energy and put it into symbols. The majority of symbols that exist today were created long ago. Over time, they have acquired layers of increasingly complex meaning.

The oldest signs with meaning are the dot and the line or egg and sperm. They are the ancestors from which all others have evolved. A dot can be expanded to form a circle that can be bisected by a vertical or horizontal line to create 'two from one' or represent the horizon. A dot can have lines drawn through its center to represent the four or eight compass points that forms a cross or asterisk or star pattern used represent Heaven, Star, God or King.

The line, drawn with a single stroke, can be vertical, horizontal and diagonal; either straight, wavy or zigzag. The vertical line is the active, dynamic principle, the body erect. The horizontal line represents the passive, static principle, the body supine. The oblique line is halfway between the vertical and the horizontal. A wavy line and a zigzag are not the same. A wavy line is fluid and passive; the zigzag is sharp, jagged and abrupt.

All symbols are designed using these seven basic shapes, variations of the dot and line. These shapes have been passed down to us through the ages and are expressed in what we call the letters of the alphabet. These were the secret signs of the shaman who wrote them in the air with a finger or a wand and painted them on rocks, animal skins and wood, but never used them as a written language. So, it is through the practice of marking that the development of all writing systems can be traced.

The practice of marking is thought to have begun around 70,000 BCE with the inscribing of dots and lines into wood, bone and stone with a purposefully sharpened instrument called a stylus or pen. These incised objects are called mnemonic devices or memory aids. Better known as talking sticks, tally sticks and message sticks, they carried numerical information such as how many days travelled, how many animals traded or how many dead. At their most complex, these devices carried detailed information on the lunar and solar calendar. They are the origin of the measuring stick or ruler.

After examining hundreds of Ice Age cave sites across Europe, paleo-archeologist Genevieve von Petzinger discovered that our ancestors used 32 signs repeatedly. The oldest of which, a red disc the size of a saucer, is estimated to be at least 41,000 years old.

She compiled a database of geometric signs found at the 370 rock sites situated across Europe. The use of these signs spanned 30,000 years of human habitation and sign-making. She also suggests that 32 of the many geometric signs accompanying such painting are repeated and combined in such a way that they could be understood as messages or even incantations.

These Ice Age signs were the origin of the pictogram and ideogram. Pictograms represent objects such as the sun, water, trees, animals, buildings, tools and weapons, or actions like run, carry, etc. Ideograms are signs that represent an idea like creation, life, eternity, day, night, halt, give, receive, think.

The oldest known pictograms date from 8500 to 4500 BCE, when they began to replace picture writing as the dominant form of visual communication. Called Vinca writing, Old European script, Balkan script or Danube script, they were created by a Neolithic people living around Vinca in Romania. The signs are found on a number of artefacts called the Tartaria Tablets, found in Tartaria in Transylvania.

Academics believe the pre-historic writing system of the Vinca was not developed for phonetic, economic or administrative reasons but as an astro-alphabet for religious ritual which gradually became increasingly complex. The script has a core of 30 abstract linear root signs expressing most of the fundamental geometric forms. The pictograms as a whole are predominantly abstract and arbitrary, rather than figurative or naturalistic motifs.

The Vinca signs bear a striking resemblance to the earliest Sumerian pictographs which are dated to 4000 BCE, five hundred years after the Vinca culture disappeared from history. It is possible that Vinca pictograms were transported as an astro-alphabet to the first civilizations of Sumer and Egypt in the form of astrolabes, star charts and zodiacs incised into clay, wood, metal and leather.

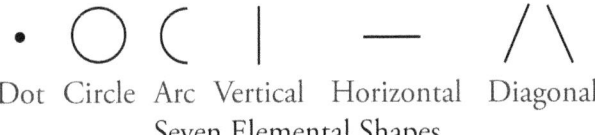

Dot Circle Arc Vertical Horizontal Diagonal
Seven Elemental Shapes

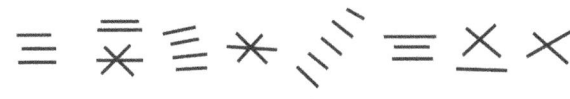

Prehistoric symbolic arrangement

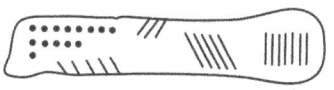

Talking stick   Tally marks   Kippu   Clay tablet   Computer tape

Mnemonic devices using dot and line arrangements for remembering numbers

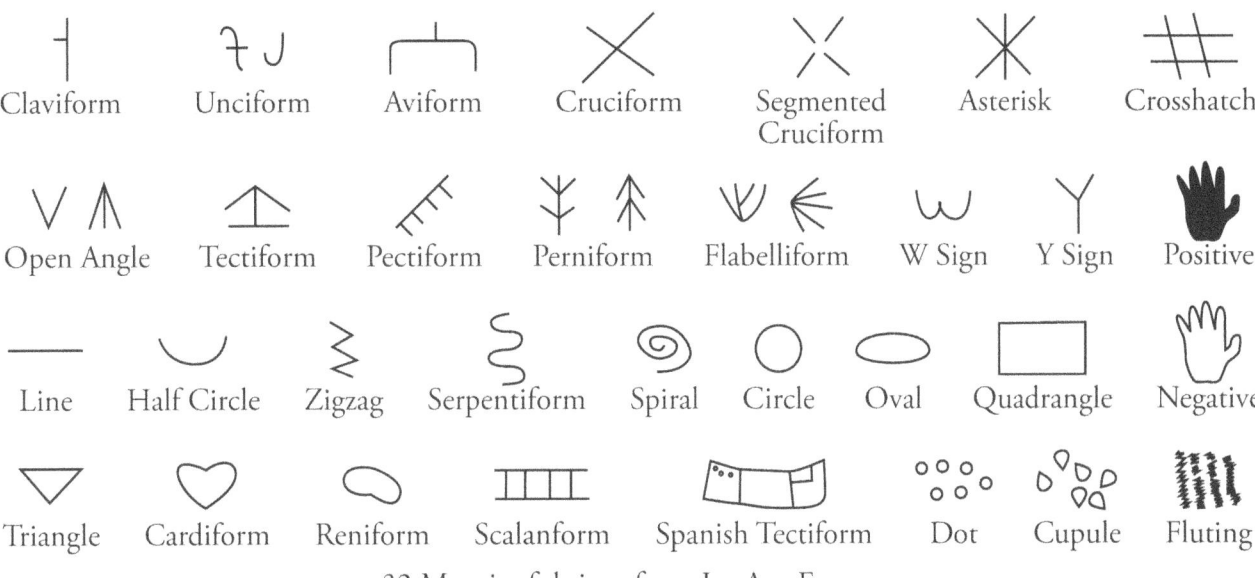

32 Meaningful signs from Ice Age Europe

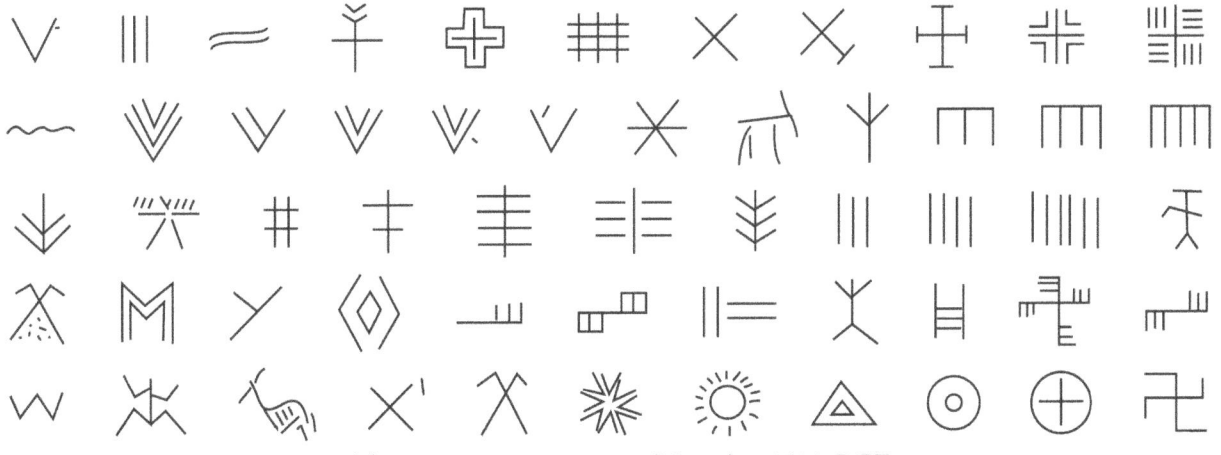

Old European pictograms (Vinca) - 5500 BCE

Universal magic symbols

Common elemental letter signs

Schema

When many different basic signs such as the cross, circle, square and triangle are overlaid on each other, the piling up of different elements produces a pattern or matrix known as a complex sign. Such a sign goes beyond its own natural expression to reveal the mysteries of the metaphysical universe.

The expression these signs produce are so complex and opaque, the compete assembled sign no longer has any expression of its own and can only be understood, not as a sign but as a schema, an underlying organisational pattern or structure.

Meaning 'shape' or 'plan', schema is a Greek term used to describe a diagrammatic representation or pattern imposed on complex reality or experience to assist in explaining it, to mediate perception or guide response. It offers a simplified abstract view of the complex reality whose proposed scope is the known and the knowable.

As a grid pattern picturing the cosmos, other signs can be formed on the schema, in which the formation of signs consists of removing some elements, so that only the remaining are made visible and recognisable.

Schema are also categorised as cosmograms, both are considered diagrammatic interpretations of the universe. They are part of the sacred geometry which, along with astronomy, astrology and alchemy, form the main metaphysical disciplines of the Hermetic knowledge developed in the Greco-Egyptian city of Alexandria from around 350 BCE onwards. Although such knowledge is much older.

Early in the first millennium, there was an explosion of interest in metaphysics. Jewish, Gnostic, Christian, Islamic and Pagan theologians all worked to uncover the order of the universe, and while different philosophers disagreed on many details, the model of the universe presented by Plato was viewed a mutual starting point. These theologians of various faiths, then set forth their own metaphysical systems, hoping to reconcile their own faith with mystical philosophy.

For all these thinkers, the natural world was seen as the unfolding of Divine Intellect. From the simplest atom to the largest galaxy, sacred geometry determines the structure and function of the universe. This was known to all ancient cultures.

In the west, it was most evident in the philosophy of the Hellenic Greeks with intellects like Pythagoras and Plato. The Greek study of mathematics and geometry were seen as foundational practices for understanding the highest principles of metaphysics or the mysteries of the universe. In studying geometry they were not learning something new but gaining an intuitive understanding of the order of the universe.

In Europe and the Middle East, this interest in metaphysics inspired the creation of schema to amplify the cosmological aspects of letters of the alphabets hidden within the construct of schema.

The Runic letters of the Norse Futhark are to be found in the schema known as the Web of the Wyrd or the Web of the Wise. While the geometric forms of the letters of the Hebrew alphabet can be found within the Star of David. Secret societies such as the Mason's, also use schema to devise various personal and cult related symbols.

Both Hindus and Buddhists have used the same principles of mathematics and geometry to generate their own schema and cosmograms in the form of mandalas and yantras.

According to Tamil tradition, the geometric forms of the Brahmi script, the parent of all modern Indian scripts, were formed on a schema or simple grid, constructed from basic geometric shapes, eight-pointed star, circle and square, to comply with phonetic rationales. The letters reflect the position of the articulatory organs, mouth, tongue, teeth, used in pronunciation.

Brahmi was used to write Sanskrit, the first documented systematic approach linking sounds in the mouth with letters. Its letters are also linked with principles and elements in nature (tatttvas), the mansions of the moon (makashastras) and the solar zodiac (rasis).

The Sanskrit system is much more than a simple ordering of letters and sounds that were used to write, read, speak and hear, it provides a system for bringing order to the cosmos. This interpretation includes breathing and yoga, which became an important factor in the structure of early alphabets.

The letters of the Sanskrit alphabet are also thought to have healing powers and are still used as sonic healing aids known as Matrika Bija.

European runes are also linked with movements in the human body in the form of runic yoga that has its roots in Bulgaria, Turkey and Russia.

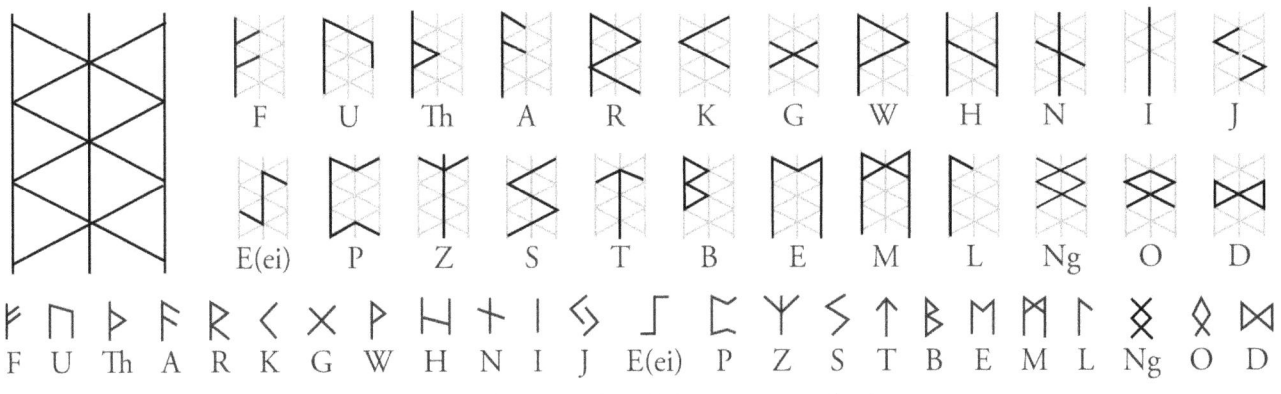

Web of the Wiyrd and the Runic Futhark

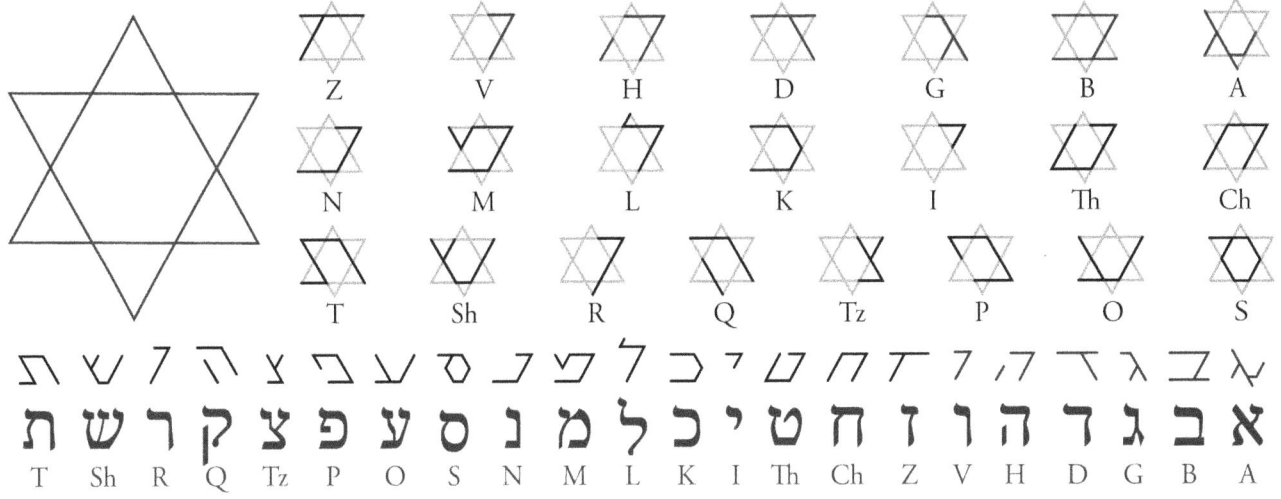

Star of David and the Hebrew Alphabet

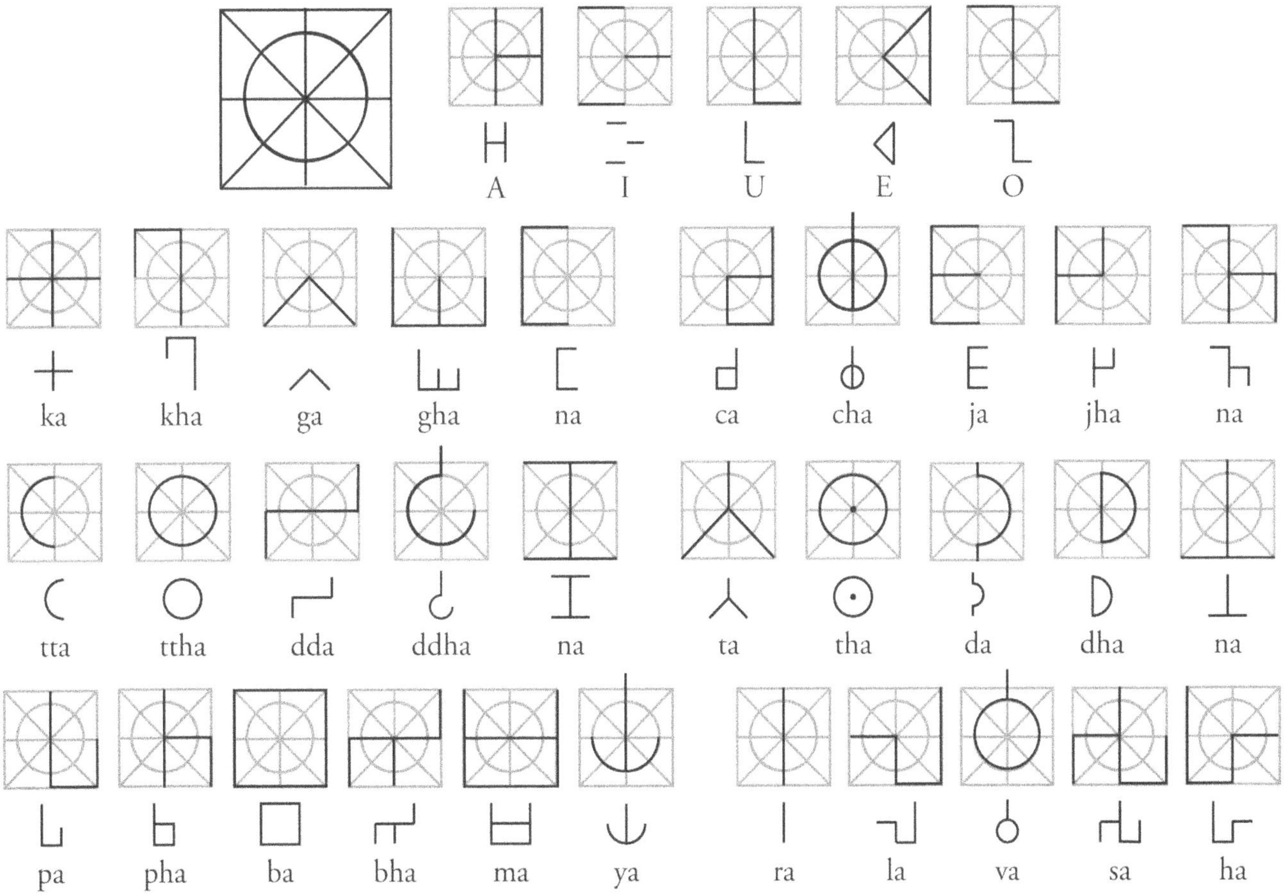

Schema for the Brahmi alphabet

Astrograms

The most recent theories on the origins of the letters of the alphabet suggest they began as 'astrograms' or star symbols used for astronomical notation in the Upper Palaeolithic era, 50,000–12,000 BCE.

The term "astrogram" is used to describe a diagram of a star constellation. When drawn, the constellations of the zodiac are astrograms but the signs of the zodiac are glyphs.

Alexander Marshacks interpretation of engraved lines as lunar calendrical notation, is one of a number of highly controversial claims made, concerning the possible astronomical significance of Upper Palaeolithic images. The claims range from lunar notation, to solstice observances in caves, to constellation representations.

It is now accepted that at least some of hunter-gather groups of the Upper Palaeolithic had detailed solstice observations, associated with the keeping of calendars and the scheduling of major ceremonies. Some hunter-gatherer groups formed "secret societies" in which esoteric astronomical knowledge was developed. The existence of calendrical notation and secluded meeting places for secret society members are suggested to be at least a plausible interpretations of Upper Palaeolithic caves and images, that maybe acted as the first temples.

The cave paintings may have represented a calendar of prey and the abstract signs may represent the lunar breeding cycle of the animals.

Other theories suggest the letters of the alphabet came about during in Neolithic times, 12,000–6000 BCE with the development of astro-alphabets found on planisphere's or star maps of the same period, some of which featured the constellations of the lunar and solar zodiacs and calendars. These theories suggest they became the foundation for the picture writing systems of the first civilisations.

Astro-alphabet theories support a very close correlation of both visual and complex theo-astrological elements between Neolithic star maps, Egyptian hieroglyphs and Hieratic script, the Phoenician, Hebrew and Ugaritic alphabets and Chinese lunar asterisms. Indicating that all early cultures typically linked the letters of the alphabet with their astronomy and cosmology, eg. stars, constellations, sun zodiac signs, lunar mansions and planets. These arrangements are linked with the stories of the skies.

In her book titled 'Alphabets of Life', Kim H Veltman explores the origins of alphabets and characters in terms of five world languages. A theme of her book is to show that the alphabetic letters, now considered abstract signs, began as cosmograms and elements to explain stories of the skies, creation and life. Beginning with an examination of the marks, signs and symbols associated with the first three stages of writing.

In Europe, this included Slavic petroglyphs, mangas and runes that marked the eternal cycles, primal forces and key moments of the annual solstices and equinoxes. Some of these became letters, often parts or subsets became letters. They also became early calendars.

In the case of Sanskrit, it is much more than a simple ordering of letters and sounds that were used to write, read, speak and hear, it provides a system for bringing order to the cosmos. Its letters are linked with principles and elements in nature (tatttvas), with the mansions of the moon (makashastras) and the zodiac of the sun (rasis).

Steven E. Franklyn theorised that the earliest characters of the Phoenician alphabet were spelled out in alphabetical order from the stars that continue to make up the lunar zodiacs of Arabia and India. The letters begin with A in Taurus and end with T in Aquarius. This totalled 19 signs, the Phoenicians needed 22 signs for their phonetic alphabet, so he suggests that Z, Ch and Th are simple variations on other letters with similar sounds and were added later.

The reason for this use, could be due to the fact that non-literate people could memorise and retain a sequence of simplified letter forms that correlated with common astronomical signs such as those of the zodiac. This could explain why pictograms of the same mnemonic value were used in place of abstract, astronomical characters.

Other scholars have written on the same subject including Peller, Meir, Wei, Marshall, Moran and Kelly, who theorise of an astronomical/zodiacal template for the alphabet. The astro-alphabet pattern has letter couplets formed from the constellations of the lunar zodiac which are also found in the Chinese lunar zodiac.

The association between the sequential lunar months and the letters of the alphabet would go some way to explain how the Norse and the Celts were so easily able to convert their lunar, tree calendars to act as an alphabet for the writing of speech.

Lunar Notation   Hunting Magic   Planisphere's - star map / zodiac

Astronomical Notation from Stone Age Europe 25,000 - 5,000 BCE

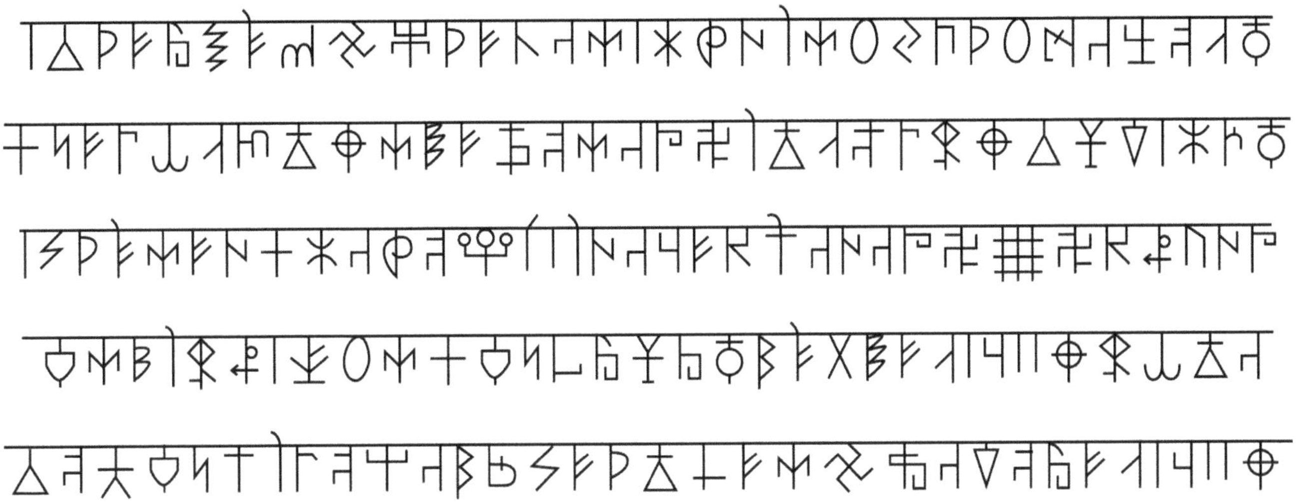

Runic Astronomical Notation - Eastern Europe

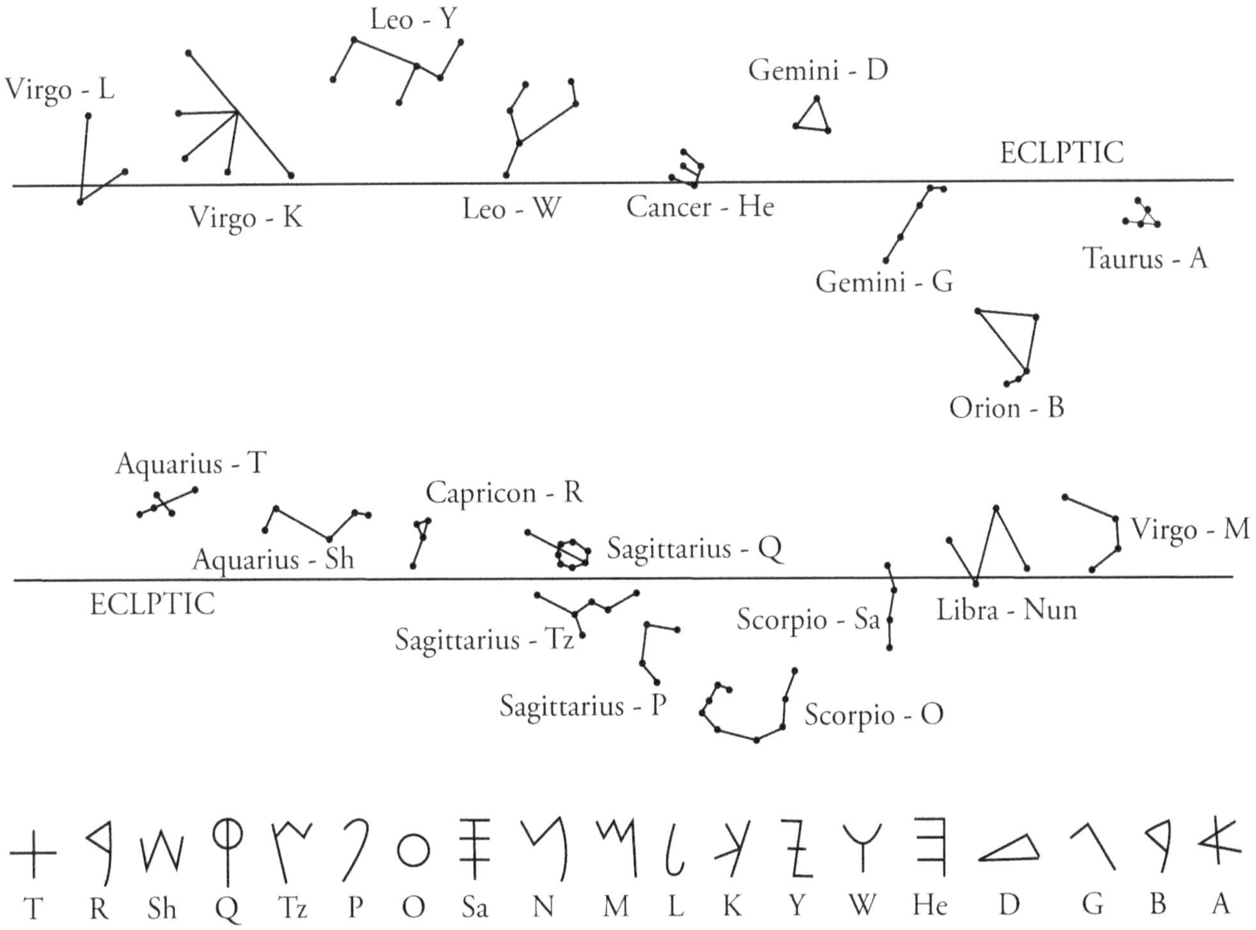

Astrograms of the lunar zodiac constellations and the Phoenician 'phonetic' alphabet

Gods of Writing

According to the Bible, mankind spoke one language known as Adamic, before the confusion of tongues at the Tower of Babel. This incident is thought to have occurred some 500 years before the emergence of the first civilizations with their separate languages and individual scripts.

The invention of writing and the alphabet has been considered an act of magic since ancient times. Most if not all religions of ancient civilizations claim that writing was originally a gift from God. His aim was to supply man with a system of communication, to record for posterity all of God's wisdom and knowledge for the benefit of all mankind. An overview of these myths reveals three main characters involved in the story of writing and alphabets.

Firstly, a supernatural being, a god of wisdom who invented writing and taught the arts of magic, divination, astrology and alchemy to man. Secondly, a supernatural or human scribe of the gods, referred to as a 'son of God', whose job it was to record God's wisdom and knowledge and chronicle the events taking place in the Garden of Eden. Thirdly, a historic human, a king or wise man, who took their inspiration from nature. Wherever these characters occur, it is in association with wisdom, knowledge, writing, alphabets, magic, calendars, poetry and business.

The first recognized civilization began in Mesopotamia around 3500 BCE, in a land called Sumer, now southern Iraq. In Sumerian mythology, the civilizing 'magician' god of wisdom called EA, meaning 'house of water' invented writing.

Later in history, the Babylonians worshipped EA using the name Enki (meaning 'Lord of Earth') as the god of wisdom and inventor of writing. Enki had a grandson called Nabu who was worshipped as the scribe of the gods. His female counterpart was called Tashmentrum/Nisaba/Nibada. She showed him how to sharpen a reed to use as a stylus.

The ancient Egyptian civilization is thought to have begun around 3100 BCE. They credited the Moon God Thoth as the inventor of hieroglyphic writing. Thoth was pictured as a man's body with an ibis' head and sometimes as a baboon because the Egyptians believed that baboons also used signs. The female aspect of Thoth called Seshet was worshipped as a goddess of measurement and the calendar.

Thoth is said to be the origin of the Greco/Roman god of writing, Hermes/Mercury. As the messenger of the gods, he is credited with the invention of the alphabet.

In Iron Age Europe, the Germanic tribes revered the god Odin as the inventor of their magical writing system called Runes. The Celts worshipped their god of eloquence called Ogmois/Oghma as the inventor of Ogham script, also called 'fairy writing', which he used to record poetry.

The Indus civilization of India began around 2500 BCE. In the Hindu religion of India there are various deities associated with writing and the alphabet. Ganesh the four-armed, elephant-headed god of wisdom is credited with the invention of writing. He was so eager to learn how to write that he broke off one of his tusks to use as a stylus to write down the dictation of Vyasa. Sarasvati is the river goddess of poetry who is credited with the invention of the alphabet.

Kali is a fearsome goddess of destruction, pictured wearing the necklace of severed human heads that represent the 52 sounds of Vedic Sanskrit in the form of the Varnamala of Bija or Garland of Letters with which Kali destroys, re-creates and preserves the universe.

Hindu's believe that Sanskrit is the dynamic language of the goddess, each letter represents a feminine energy (Shakti), a form of Kali. Therefore, she is seen as the mother of all language, of all bija, mantra and shashtra.

Chinese civilization is dated to around 2200 BCE. In Chinese mythology, Fu Xi was an emperor god who taught the ways of civilization to man. He invented both writing and the I-Ching, taking his inspiration from symbols found carved into the shell of a sacred turtle.

In Central America, a tall, white, bearded man, referred to as a winged or feathered serpent, was responsible for the spread of civilization and literacy throughout the continent. He was known by many names, including Votan and Quetzalcoatl.

Scribes of the Gods

Of all the gods connected with the invention of writing, Thoth is the one most associated with the invention of the letters of the alphabet. In Egypt, he was known as Djehuty, the Phoenicians called him Taautos, the Alexandrians knew him as Thouth and the Mycenae Greeks called him Thoth. He was known as Hermes by the Hellenic Greeks, and Mercury by the Romans. In medieval times, he was the composite magician, Thoth/Hermes/Mercury, known as Hermes Trismegistus, the Thrice Great Hermes, founder of Hermeticism.

There are many biblical, mythological and historical works that recall his association with writing and the alphabet, stretching back to the Hebrew Patriarchs of Eden.

Enoch was a direct descendent of Adam, seventh in the patriarchal bloodline, son of Jared, father of Methuselah and great grandfather of Noah. He was taught to write by the Fallen Angel, Penume, who first taught writing to mankind.

Enoch was considered to be a man of integrity, being educated and truthful. For this reason, he was chosen by God to work as his scribe, under the tutelage of the Archangel Uriel (Enki?), to record the comings and goings of gods and man in the Garden of Eden. He was deified as the scribe of the gods, rewarded with eternal life for his work, becoming the archetype for later scribal gods such as Nabu, Thoth, Hermes, Mercury and Hermes Trismegistus.

Nabu was the Babylonian scribe of the gods, the grandson of Enki, the god of wisdom and the inventor of writing. In Babylonian art, Nabu is pictured holding a clay tablet and a triangular stylus. Babylonian myth tells how Nabu invented writing and used it as a kind of net to trap all of God's knowledge on clay tablets. His wife, Tashmetrum, showed him how to sharpen a reed to use as a stylus.

In ancient Egypt, the Moon God Djehuty/Thoth, the oldest son of the Sun God Ra and keeper of his father's wisdom and knowledge, was the 'Lord of Holy Words', the patron of scribes.

He was credited with the invention of many things including writing and numbers. He was considered a god of learning, of mathematics, science, magic, sacred texts and controlling space and time. The female aspect of Thoth, called Seshet, was worshipped as a goddess of measurement and the calendar.

Thoth performed many tasks for the gods, including reforming the calendar from lunar to solar; and following the confusion of tongues at the building of the Tower of Babel, creating the new languages of man and scripts to write them.

In Egyptian art, Thoth was pictured as a man's body with the head of an ibis, and sometimes as a baboon because the Egyptians believed that baboons also used signs.

He is most famously depicted with the head of an ibis because the ibis is the Egyptian equivalent of the Greek crane, the birds who inspired the Greek god of writing, Hermes, to invent wedge-shaped letter forms, *"as birds fly in a V formation making letters in the sky."*

According to the Phoenician writer, Sanchuriathon, the divine Bronze Age scribe called Taautos of Byblos was the inventor of letters. Taautos was bequeathed the land of Egypt by Cronus. He was believed to have lived before the Trojan War and belonged to the snake priesthood. He also wrote the work called The Commentaries in which he discussed Creation.

Greek myth tells that Thouth/Thoth/Hermes was the inventor of the alphabet who shared his invention with the Egyptians and Phoenicians to help them in their efforts to create a simple method of transcribing business administration in their international trade dealings between each other and the Babylonians and Assyrians.

The Romans claim their messenger god Hermes/Mercury brought the alphabet with him from Greece to Italy where his mother, the nymph Carmenta, adapted it to write the Latin language.

In the late Middle Ages, 12th century CE, Thoth, Hermes and Mercury became the composite magician known as Hermes Trismegistus or the Thrice Great Hermes, author of The Hermetica, the foundation of astrology, alchemy and sacred geometry.

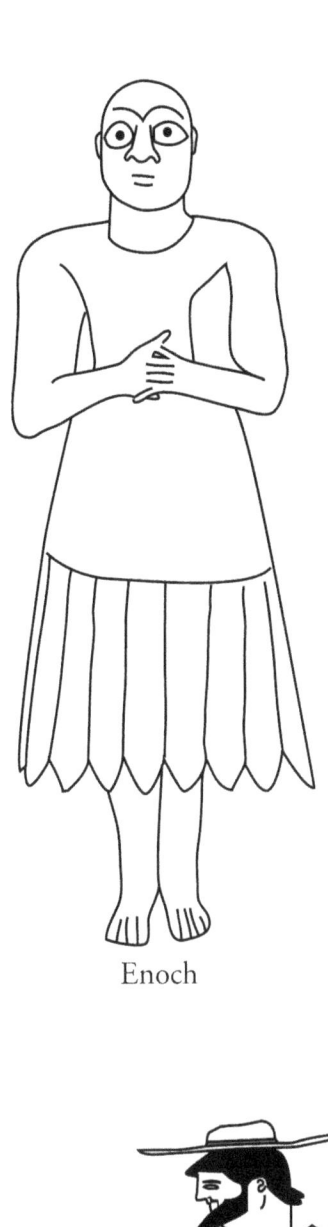
Enoch

Nabu

Djehuty / Taautos / Thouth / Thoth

Hermes

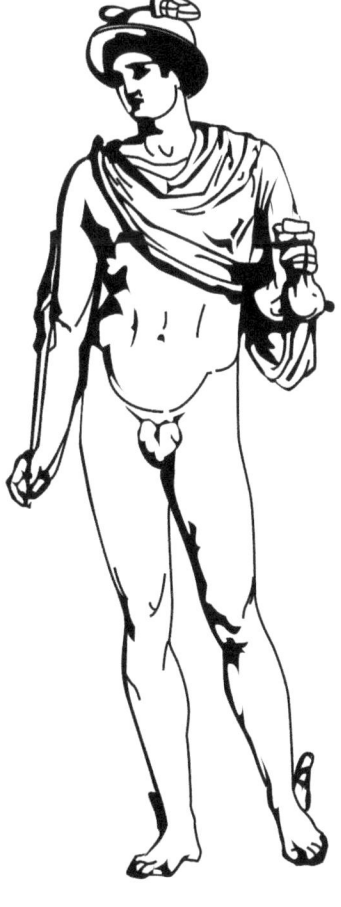
Mercury

Hermes Trismegistus

Numbers, Letters, Numerals

Number mysticism is an integral part of an occult alphabet and the writing of numbers is thought to have an integral influence on the development of writing and the alphabet. In many archaic cultures, accounting was associated with primitive forms of recording. There is compelling evidence to suggest that writing grew out of accounting; meaning that, ,theoretically at least, numeracy preceded literacy.

It is considered that during this truly archaic period, all the basic geometric shapes were discovered and systemized into early man's spiritual belief system. By using dots to count and represent numbers and arranging the dots in certain patterns or arrays and joining them with straight lines, they formed simple and compiles geometric shapes.

In Jewish cabalistic theory, it is thought that the letter-numbers of the Hebrew alphabet represent the regular polygons that can be found within a circle, from the triangle 3, followed by the square 4, the pentagon 5, hexagon 6, up to the 360-degree polygon.

In ancient times, the success of the primitive, archaic number system relied on its use of iterative stroke notation, in which the number of strokes corresponds to the number expressed, i.e. one stroke for 1, two strokes for 2, three strokes for 3, etc., to form iconic patterns that act as a memory aid. This form of numerical representation remained the most popular method of recording numbers under 10, as is shown by its continued use by all early advanced civilizations.

The Mayans of Central America employed an iterative system of dots and lines arranged horizontally for numbers under 19 and vertically for numbers 20 and above. They were the only ancient civilization to use zero as a number, represented by the glyph of a conch shell.

To reduce the inconvenience of iconic notation when dealing with large numbers, new signs were invented for higher number values. Elementary signs were developed for 5, 10, 100, 1000 and larger.

A sign that represents a number is called a numeral. The numerals I, V, X, are older than any alphabet. They are thought to be descended directly from making notches on tally sticks used by herdsmen. I is a representation of a finger, V is 5 fingers of one hand, and X is the 10 fingers of both hands crossed.

While the Egyptians still used picture signs or hieroglyphs to represent numbers, the Minoan civilization of Crete, 2000–1400 BCE, employed a series of linear signs representing the elementary number values of base 10, from 1 to 100.

Following the invention of the alphabet, the innovative idea of using letters as numbers was perfected by the Greek mathematician Pythagoras in the 7th century BCE. This system is said to be the descendant of the ancient, secret number magic of the Chaldeans and Babylonians, inherited by the Greeks and Hebrews.

In his alpha-numeric system, the alphabet uses its letter order A–Z to represent the ordinal numbers 1 to 26, and the cardinal numbers or multiples of 10 to 90 and 100 to 900 with no sign for zero. Alexander the Great established the use of this alpha-numeric system throughout his empire which stretched from Greece to Egypt, through Babylon and Persia to Pakistan. Thereby establishing the international link between numerology and the alphabet that became an integral part of cabala during the 1st century CE.

The Greeks also invented acrophonic numerals. Meaning 'initial sound', the acrophonic principle allows a number to be represented by the initial letter of its name. In Greek, this meant that D, the first letter of Decca the word for 10, represented the number 10. This principle is considered to be a useful memory aid for teaching numeracy and literacy.

The acrophonic system combines signs to make other numbers not represented. When a letter is preceded by a one of lesser numerical value, e.g. IX, it signifies the subtraction of the smaller number from the larger number. When a letter is followed by a letter of smaller numerical value, e.g. VI or XVI, it signifies the addition of the numbers. The inconvenience of this notation system is that it requires multiple repetitions of identical symbols, i.e. XXXVIIII = 39.

The modern European number system known as Arabic numerals were once letters in an obscure Indo-Bactrian alphabet from the 7th century BCE. With the invention of the zero, this Indian system only requires ten signs ranging from 0 to 9 to write all other numbers. It was adopted by Arab mathematicians in the 8th century who introduced it into Europe during the 12th and 13th centuries, where it quickly replaced the cumbersome Roman acrophonic system. Thus evolved the separation between our alphabetic signs and our numerals.

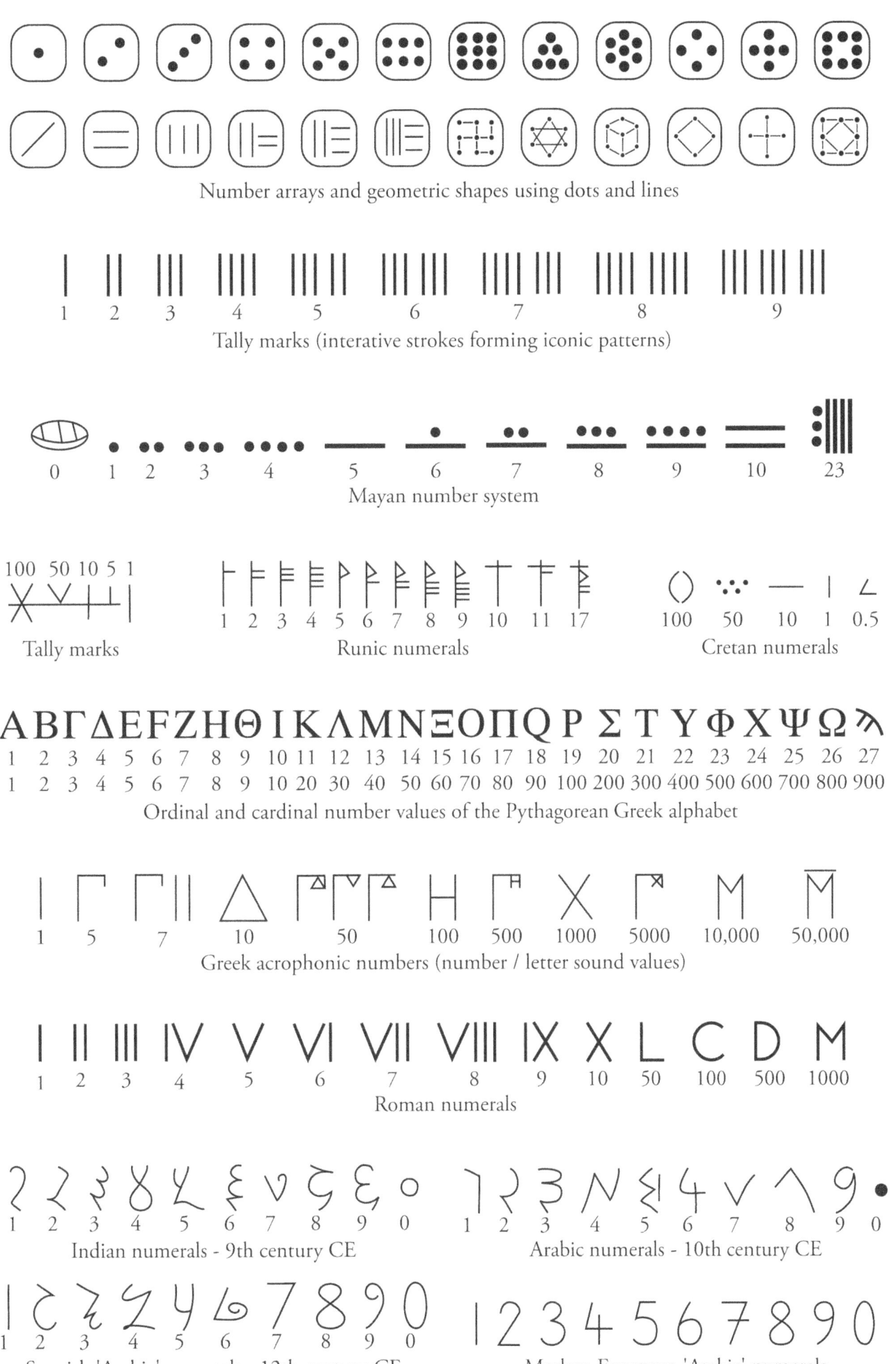

Ancient Writing

The magic of writing lays its use of picture signs to express human thoughts and language. Astronomical notation produced powerful symbols whose ancestors feature in the abstract symbolism of Stone Age European cave art, zodiacs and star maps. It is considered these systems had the capacity to act as written scripts for conveying short messages, prayers, incantations and spells.

By 5000 BCE, picture writing was a global activity which is one reason why it is wrongly thought to be the origin of writing itself. The difference between the two being, picture writing is highly illustrative and communicates the message as a whole image, whilst writing uses individual stylised symbols to represent individual segments of human speech to record language.

Picture writing is essentially a drawing of things and acts (deeds, actions, etc), helped out by heraldic indications of proper names and by strokes and dots to represent days and distances and other such quantitative ideas.

In the Native American picture writing tradition, the first example shows a letter written by "Turtle following his wife" to his son "little man". It says he was sending $53 dollars and asking him to return home. The second example, tells of a journey by Chief Kingfisher, taking 3 days using 5 canoes accompanied by spirit creatures, eagle, snake and lizard. The turtle represents his safe homecoming.

Academics believe that proto writing proper began around 6000 BCE, when Neolithic farmers living in Mesopotamia (Iraq), began to use trade tokens or molded clay figures to represent the goods that farmers traded, i.e. 3 jars of oil for 1 sheep. To make trading fairer, the farmer trading the oil would place three 'oil' tokens inside a clay envelope and inscribe the number and the shape of the oil tokens on to the outer surface of the clay envelope. It was left to dry in the sun to be used as an early form of receipt.

When the trade was made, the clay envelope was broken open and the trade tokens were used to confirm what was inscribed on the envelope. As the convenience of this system was realized, the tokens were discarded and their graphic representation and number written on to flat tablets of damp clay using a reed stylus. This system also allowed for more than one item of information to be held on one tablet of clay. To prevent confusion all the individual transactions were separated by the use of lines, this is the beginnings of writing as we know it.

At first, picture signs were only used to write words to form simple sentences such as 'five sheep' or 'man kill lion'. This method of recording language or writing is called pictographic script. It emerged around 3300 BCE in Mesopotamia and marks the beginning of writing proper.

Pictograms are simplified picture signs representing object and action words like sun, moon, star, sheep, lion, boat, run, sit, sleep, etc. Another form of pictogram is the ideogram or idea sign, a simplified picture or abstracted sign representing an idea such as day, night, bright, horizon, up, down, east, west, etc.

But the most important development in writing was the realization that a sign could be used to represent a sound that bore no resemblance to its pictographic meaning. For instance, the pictograms for "bee" and "leaf" could be combined together to write the word "belief", an abstract concept with no concrete object to represent it.

The use of pictograms as sound puns is called Rebus writing. It is thought that Rebus writing was developed mainly for the writing of the king's name and this enabled the development of syllabic script. To achieve this, pictograms underwent a process of phonetic and graphic reduction. Phonetically, the Rebus principle enabled a pictogram that represented a word to represent a unit of speech called a syllable. Early syllable forms were three letter sounds such as til, mai, nun, etc. At some point the last letter was dropped to leave ti, ma, nu, etc., for more accurate communication.

The necessity to write quickly led to a graphic reduction, the simplification or abstraction of picture signs into what we call letters. In some cases, such as cuneiform or Chinese characters, the abstraction was so great they created a new form of sign called logograms.

The major problem with logo-syllabic script is that it is a complex system; it not only requires a sign for every syllable used in a language but it also requires extra signs called determinatives and phonetic compliments to help determine the true meaning of a word or phrase. This led to the huge abecedaries of the ancient world that contained hundreds, even thousands of signs. So, a simpler one sign - one sound system or alphabet was created by dropping the last letter of a syllable to create a phoneme i.e., Nun, Nu, N.

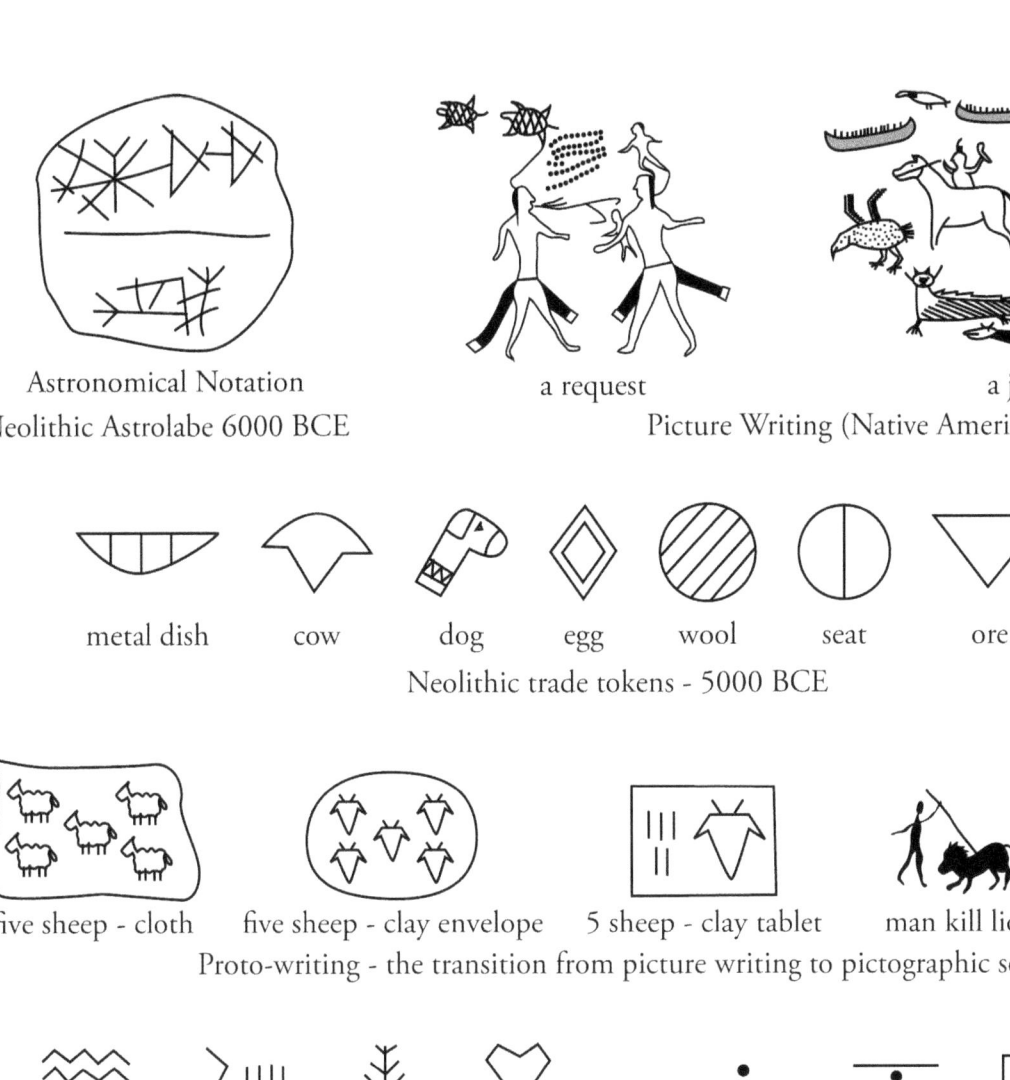

Astronomical Notation
Neolithic Astrolabe 6000 BCE

a request   a journey
Picture Writing (Native American)

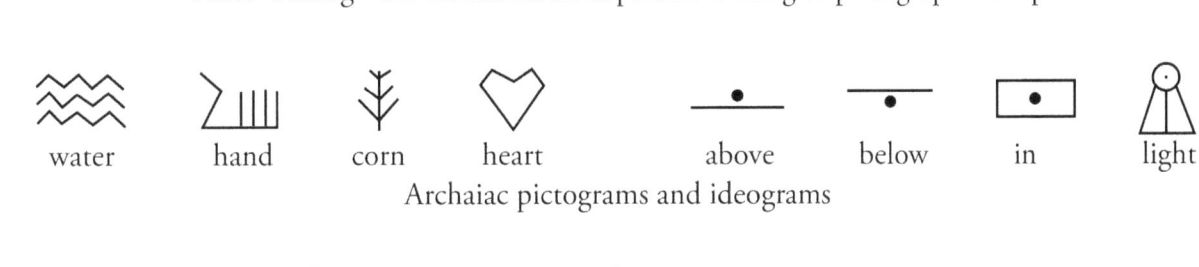

metal dish   cow   dog   egg   wool   seat   ore   oil
Neolithic trade tokens - 5000 BCE

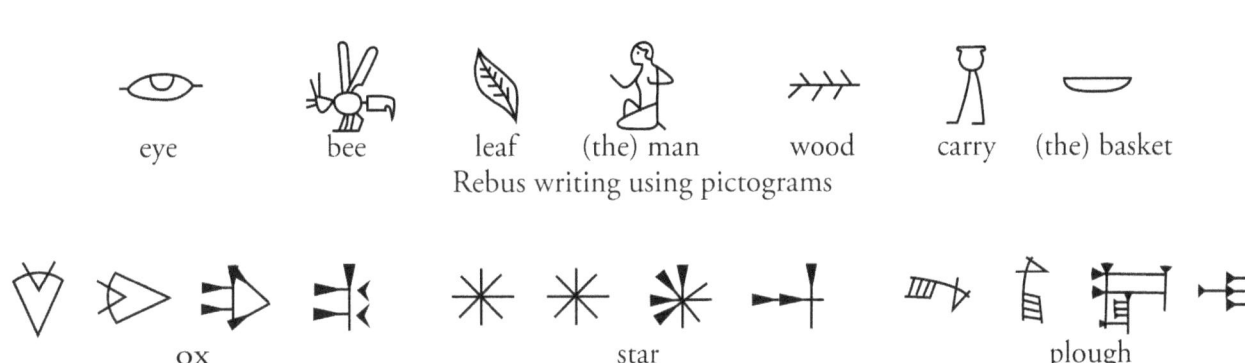

five sheep - cloth   five sheep - clay envelope   5 sheep - clay tablet   man kill lion   man kill lion
Proto-writing - the transition from picture writing to pictographic script

water   hand   corn   heart   above   below   in   light
Archaiac pictograms and ideograms

eye   bee   leaf   (the) man   wood   carry   (the) basket
Rebus writing using pictograms

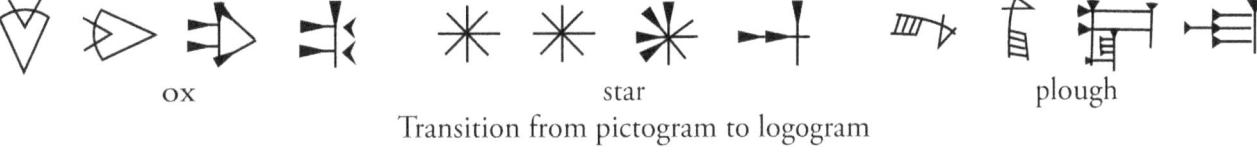

ox   star   plough
Transition from pictogram to logogram

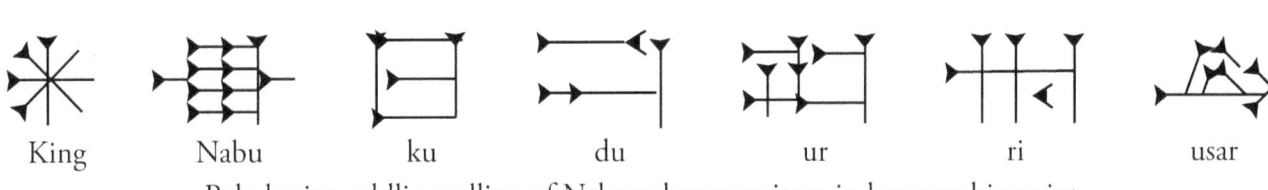

King   Nabu   ku   du   ur   ri   usar
Babylonian sybllic spelling of Nebucadnezer written in logographic script

Ox/Aleph   Ah   A   Water/Mem   Mm   M   Head/Resh   Rsh   R   Sign/ Tav   Ta   T
Phonetic and graphic reduction of picture letters by the acrophonic principle

Ancient Scripts

Recognized as a gift of the gods, writing was and still is revered through its sacred scripts. Each civilization developed its own script style, defined by the writing mediums used. These mediums included a chisel and stone, a reed stylus and damp clay, a reed brush or pen and papyrus – the first paper, thereby creating the three ancient individual writing styles of cuneiform, hieroglyphs and picto-linear script, the parent of alphabetic script.

Each civilization used a monumental script, alphabetic signs carved into stone with a chisel for writing proclamations and edicts. To write scripture and law in books required the use of a less time-consuming, less expensive form of script called cursive linear script or handwriting.

The Sumerians of Mesopotamia were the world's first civilization. They are credited with the invention of the wheel and writing. They first drew pictograms in damp clay with the pointed end of a reed from around 3300 BCE. Then, around 3100 BCE, for some unexplained reason, the scribes turned the stylus on its end and began to use the wider, triangular end of the reed stylus, impressing it into the damp clay to create wedge-shaped renditions of their pictographic writing forms.

These wedge-shaped marks developed into a logographic writing system called cuneiform, a Latin term meaning 'wedge-shaped'. It was used to write phonetic units of sound called syllables to form words and write sentences. There are several distinct forms produced by the Sumerians, Akkadians, Babylonians, Assyrians and Persians.

The cumbersome cuneiform system was quickly replaced as the dominant writing system across the Middle East around 700 BCE by the Aramaic variant of the Phoenician alphabet.

By 3100 BCE, the ancient Egyptians had developed their picture signs into the famous hieroglyphic script. In the early stages of development there were about 700 glyphs in use. By 1500 BCE, scribes had developed around 24 bi and uni-consonant glyphs to write the Egyptian language, almost creating the world's first one sign – one sound writing system. This abecedary of signs is often referred to as the Egyptian alphabet. However, new symbols were constantly being invented and by 500 BCE, they numbered several thousand.

The Egyptians are famous for carving their hieroglyphs in stone. Scribes also wrote hieroglyphs on papyrus with a reed brush or pen dipped in black ink or red ink for the names of gods. The invention of ink, reed brush and papyrus, enabled the Egyptians to develop the first formal cursive script called 'hieratic', a Greek term meaning 'priestly', a simplified version of hieroglyphs.

Written horizontally from right to left, hieratic script came into use around 2500 BCE, a time when hieroglyphs were only used for the writing of sacred texts. By 1750 BCE it had developed into a distinctive cursive script in its own right. Its use as a script peaked in the New Kingdom (1550–1330 BCE) and ended around the end of the 1st century CE.

In the eastern Mediterranean, from 2000 BCE onwards, picto-linear scripts were developed in Crete and Cyprus. These simplified and abstracted linear forms are thought to have influenced the Egyptians and the Phoenicians in their development of a simplified writing system for international trading purposes.

For a brief period around 2000 BCE, Phoenician merchants wrote a picto-linear script called 'Gubalitic', after Gubal, the Phoenician name for the city called Byblos by the Greeks. It employed 120 distinct signs which discounts it as an alphabet. It is classified as 'pseudo-hieroglyphic', implying that it was influenced by Egyptian hieratic script, but some of the signs resemble Cretan Linear A script. It isn't known whether the Gubalitic script had any influence on either the phonetic or graphic development of the alphabet, as it remains undeciphered.

In 660 BCE, Egyptian scribes developed a less formal, practical handwriting called 'demotic'. Its origin and derivation from hieratic script is not fully understood, but it is thought that it evolved as an administration script used in the chanceries of Upper Egypt.

Demotic replaced hieratic for the writing of letters and documents in administration as it was more cursive than hieratic and as a 'running' script (cursive, flowing handwriting) it was used on soft surfaces such as mummy wrappings.

Around 200 BCE, Greek became the official language of Egypt under the rule of the Alexander the Great and the hieroglyphic, hieratic and demotic scripts gradually disappeared from use, replaced by Greek, then Arabic forms of the alphabet. The last use of demotic script dates to 470 CE.

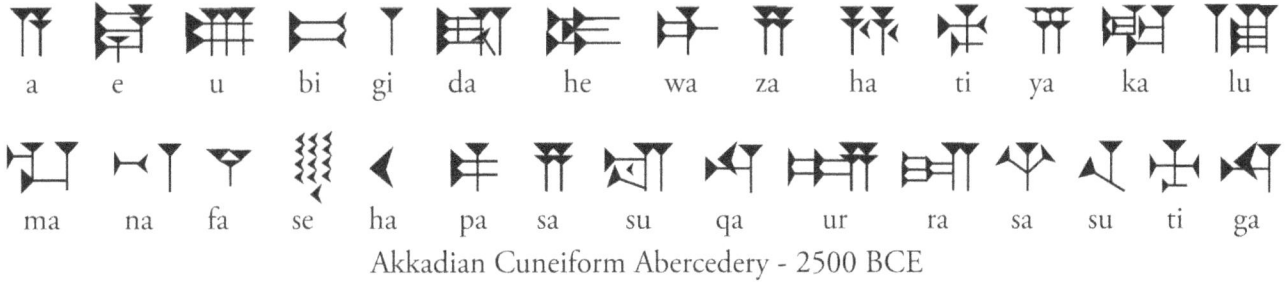

Akkadian Cuneiform Abercedery - 2500 BCE

Old Persian Cuneiform Abercedery - 500 BCE

Logographic Scripts

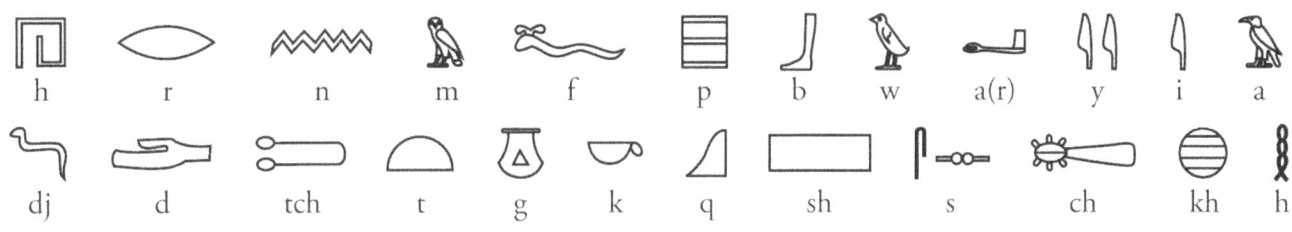

Egyptian syllabic and initial sounds expressed by pictograms and ideograms

Hieroglyphic alphabet - 1500 BCE

Development of the sign for Scribe from Hieroglyph to Hieratic and Demotic script

Hieratic script - 1750 BCE

Phoenician Gublitic script - 2000 BCE

Demotic script - 660 BCE

Linear Scripts

Phoenician Alphabet

The Phoenician alphabet is regarded as the parent of all modern alphabets. The idea of an alphabetic script or one sign – one sound system of writing was perfected from syllabic script over a period lasting from around 1500–800 BCE by the Egyptians, Phoenicians and Greeks, to create the first alphabet as we know it.

The Phoenicians were a Semitic-speaking people living in Canaan (modern Lebanon). They were merchants who supplied the Egyptians with papyrus, the first paper, from their city of Gubal, which the Greeks called Byblos, the origin of the words Bible and book. With influences from Egypt and Crete, they invented the adjad or consonant-only alphabet to simplify their international business transactions with Egypt, Babylon, Assyria and Greece.

The Phoenician adjad was formed of 22 linear signs based on existing pictograms, that used cursive script or handwriting to write, from right to left, the 22 consonant sounds used to speak the Semitic language.

To create the first one sign – one sound system, it is surmised that the Phoenicians dropped the last letter of syllables, ti, ma, nu, to leave the single letter sounds, t, m, n, etc. They are also thought to have attached the signs to the sounds by applying the acrophonic principle, enabling a sound to be represented by a sign whose initial letter of its name begins with the sound represented, i.e. A = Apple, B = Boat, C = Cat, etc. It isn't understood whether this mnemonic method was chosen for its simplicity or if it was an adaptation of an already existing system or whether it had religious connotations.

Archeologists claim the first stage in the development of the Phoenician alphabet is present in a small selection of dedications to the gods inscribed on small statuettes. This pictographic script, called Proto-Sinaitic, was employed circa 1900 BCE, when it is thought that Semite slaves working in the salt mines of the Sinai Peninsula adapted Egyptian hieroglyphs to write the Semitic language, using their own special set of linear pictograms, as some of the Proto-Sinaitic pictograms appear in a simpler form in later versions. These forms led to the creation of the Old Semitic linear script which first appeared around 1700 BCE.

Ugaritic cuneiform script is often referred to as the first alphabet and the Phoenician letter order seems to have been inherited from it. Ugaritic was a Semitic language spoken in the Syrian port of Ugarit. The script seems to have emerged suddenly, at some point before 1400 BCE. It employed 30 cuneiform logograms of East Semitic, Akkadian-Babylonian origin, that correspond to the consonants used to write the West Semitic family of languages to which Ugaritic, Phoenician, Hebrew and Aramaic belong.

The Old Semitic linear script was adapted to the North Semitic writing system that emerged in Syria around 1500 BCE. It is the earliest fully developed writing system, ancestral to the Phoenician and Aramaic alphabets. It had 22 letters representing consonants only, that were written right to left. These characteristics are typical of most of the later Semitic alphabets, like those of the Hebrews and Arabs.

Around 1200 BCE, North Semitic linear script was adapted to the West Semitic dialect, appearing as an early Canaanite script, sometimes called Old Phoenician. By 1050 BCE, the Phoenicians had perfected the Canaanite letters into a linear script of 22 signs, arranged in order, to write the 22 consonant sounds of the Phoenician language from right to left. This alphabet is called the Byblian alphabet, named after the Phoenician port of Byblos/Gubal.

The Phoenician writing system proved so successful it was adapted to write other Semitic languages, Aramaic, Hebrew, Moabite, Samaritan, Syriac and Arabic. It was also adapted by Indo-European-speaking peoples, particularly the Persians, Greeks and Romans.

The writing of Semitic languages does not require the writing of vowels to be readable. If needed, they are represented by diacritic marks, placed above and below the letters in a word to indicate pronunciation. In Indo-European languages such as Greek and Latin, the vowels are a necessary requirement to indicate meaning such as gender, tense, plurality, etc.

Around 800 BCE, the Greeks adapted certain Semitic consonant sounds not used in the Greek language, to represent the vowel sounds of the Greek language, thereby creating the first true alphabetic writing system of consonants and vowels.

The Greek alphabet was taken to Italy around 500 BCE where it was adapted to write Latin, to become the model for all modern European alphabets.

Egyptian hieroglyphs (top) and their derivative Proto-Siniatic pictograms - 1900 BCE

Old Semitic - 1700 BCE

Ugaritic Cuneiform (West Semitic) - 1600 BCE

North Semitic - 1500 BCE

West Semituc / Canaanite / Early Phonecian - 1200 BCE

Byblian / Phoenician alphabet - 1050 BCE

Phonetic and graphic adaptation of Phoenician to the Greco-Roman alphabet

Mythological Greek Alphabet

In his book 'The White Goddess', Robert Graves theorizes about an original alphabet, whose letter order and religious secrets are still to be found in the myths concerning the Goidelic alphabet.

Derived from Greek mythology, bardic verse and the writings of various ancient historians, Graves explains that the Greeks are descended from a people called the Pelasgians, who lived in Europe before the arrival of the Greek tribes, pre-2000 BCE. It is surmised that the Pelasgians were a Hittite tribe originating from ancient Anatolia, modern Turkey, who spread westwards into Europe, populating the lands and islands of the Aegean Sea in the eastern Mediterranean.

The Pelasgians were named after their king, Pelasgus, the grandson of Deucalion, the Greek equivalent of Noah. His son was Lycaon, the first king of Arcadia, and the Greeks are named after his son Greacus. The Pelasgians were also called Dioi meaning 'divine' because they alone of all Greeks preserved the use of letters after the Deluge, incised as numbers on dice made of ox bone.

Graves theorizes that the Pelasgians are the originators of a sacred tree alphabet that existed as a religious secret of the Moon Goddess, including her secret name hidden in the five vowels.

Its letter sounds are thought to have had mnemonic names which were later shortened to Alpha, Beta, Gamma, etc. It was never written as a script, the sounds of the alphabet were marked by twigs taken from trees that represented the months of the year according to the lunar calendar, in which more secrets were hidden.

Greek myths tell that either the Three Fates, priestesses of the Moon Goddess Io, invented seven letters, five vowels A O U E I and the consonants B and T, or that Hermes invented their wedge-shaped signs after watching flights of cranes *"which make letters as they fly."* Palamedes, the son of Nauplius invented eleven others, LNFSNgHDCGPR.

This arrangement of sounds attached to wedge-shaped signs is thought to be the mythical, Pelasgian eighteen-letter alphabet of thirteen consonants BLNFSNgHDTCGPR and five vowels AOUEI. It is said that any record of this letter order and its wedge-shaped script was lost to history around 1000 BCE, following the conquest of Mycenae Greece by the Dorian Greeks.

According to Graves, the Pelasgians spoke an Aeolian/Cypriot dialect of Greek also known as Mycenae Greek and the Cretans were descended from them. He also submits that the Pelasgians took Hittite pictograms to Crete where, in Greek myth, the alphabet is said to have originated and was current in the Peloponnese before the Trojan War.

Legend tells that Hermes took the Pelasgian alphabet to Crete, where he adapted Hittite/Cretan pictograms to the sounds to write the Indo-European, Mycenae Greek language, thought to be the Linear A script. It also says he adapted the later Cretan picto-linear signs of Linear B to write Minoan. This system was, in earlier, more cumbersome forms, taken to Cyprus, Cilia and Lycia.

The myth goes on to say that Hermes altered the Pelasgian letter order before taking it to the island of Pharos, to assist the Egyptians and the Phoenicians in their search for a one sound–one sign writing system. The Phoenicians reformed it to write their Semitic language, altering the script and letter order, writing it in reverse and attaching Semitic mnemonic names to the letters.

Several centuries after the destruction of the Mycenae civilization, the Semitic variant of the Pelasgian alphabet was brought back to Greece by the Phoenician king, Cadmus, who settled in Boetia around 800 BCE. This Cadmean alphabet, with the addition of vowels and other consonants, was adapted to form the 23-letter alphabet of classic, Hellenic Greece.

Epicharmus of Sicily added Theta and Chi or Psi and Pi. Simonides added Zeta and Pi, Psi or Phi. The two vowels, Omega and Epsilon were added by the priests of Apollo, so that his sacred lyre now has one vowel for each of its seven strings. This led to the vowels being associated with the seven-letter sacred Name of God 'Jieuoao/Jehovah' and correspondences with the magic of the number 7, seven planets, seven days of the week, seven colours of the rainbow, etc.

From Greece, Cadmean letters, as they were called by the Hellenic Greeks, were taken to Italy by Evander of Arcadia, son of Mercury, where his mother, the nymph Carmenta, adapted them to write the Etruscan language.

BLNFSNgHDTCGPR AOUEI
Letter order of the Pelasgian alpabet (Robert Graves)

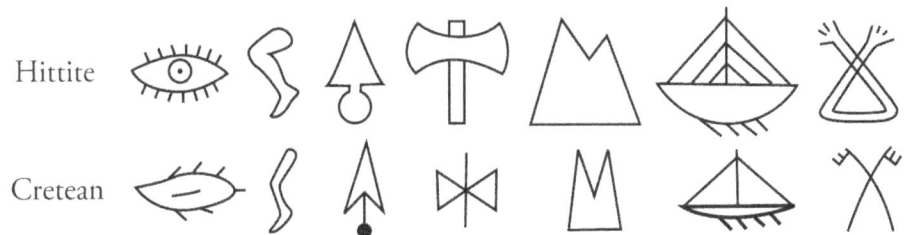

Hittite and Cretan hieroglyphs - 2000 BCE

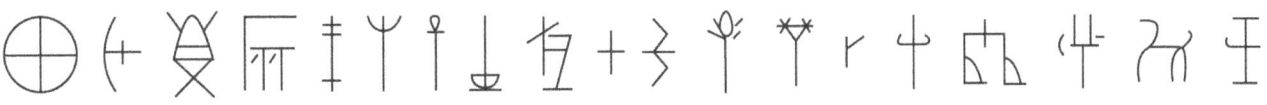

Linear A - 1800 BCE (Mycene Greek)

Linear B - 1400 BCE (Minoan Greek)

Early Hellenic Greek (Cadmean) - 800 BCE

Old Etruscan - 700 BCE

Early Roman - 600 BCE

Occult Alphabets

The occultism that is enshrined in the alphabet is entrenched in the moral philosophies and wisdoms of the ancient past, designed by the greatest spiritual and scientific minds of the time. Letters are not just simple symbols representing sounds, and numbers are not just quantities, both were designed to reveal deeper meanings to those initiated into their mysteries. Every letter acts as an illustration, an interpretation or visual explanation of itself.

The letters of the alphabet were considered sacred, believed to have been endowed with God's attributes. The actual formation of the letter shapes is attributed to the scribe of the gods. There were no vowels in the Hebrew alphabet as they are deemed too sacred to write, for they are the animating spirit of words and the sound of them speaks the true and overwhelming name of God. When the Greeks borrowed the alphabet, they added vowels to write their language.

Hebrew is written from right to left for the very special reason that God created the universe by His own reflection. By writing right to left, they were going towards the source of God. The Greeks reversed this and their alphabet was written left to right.

A letter's name, Alpha, Beta, Gamma, etc., is the mystical name of a number, revealing its hidden meaning, for the letters and numbers are completely interchangeable, making the techniques of isosephy – gematria, temurah and notariqon possible. Holy books such as the Torah and the Bible are said to be composed of various combinations of these letter-number techniques, giving important clues to the deeper meanings, also having planetary and astrological interpretations.

All of these mystical traditions are to be found in the cabalistic mysteries. The earliest initiates believed that God taught these mysteries to the angels. After the fall of man, the angels gave the secrets to Adam so that he might understand his error and gain back what he had lost. These secrets are supposed to awake in man when he studies the 10 numbers and 22 basic sounds formed from the letter combinations of God's own name. This, combined with the geometric figures that were used in designing the letters of the alphabet, the circle, square and triangle, is the basis of cabala.

Cabala supplies the key to the spiritual truths of holy books, a key which begins with a dynasty of priest-kings originating in Atlantis, known as the Melchizedek. The last of these priest-kings is said to have passed this knowledge on to Abraham, a Chaldean who passed it on down the patriarchal line through Isaac, Moses, David and Solomon. Abraham was supposed to have brought these wisdoms to Egypt where the Egyptians gained knowledge of them. Jesus was instructed in these mysteries about 600 years after Pythagoras studied there.

The 10 numbers and the 22 letters are central to the mysticism contained in the cabalistic Tree of Life. The tree as a source of wisdom is depicted in the legends of all cultures. In cabala or Jewish mysticism, the Sephirotic Tree represents inner knowing. In the Bible, there is a Tree of Life and a Tree of Knowledge, around which mankind first came into a realization of being in control of his own destiny. In pagan Europe, in the Norse tradition, Yggdrasil is the tree symbol of life, space, time and destiny. The Celts venerated trees and regarded oak groves as particularly sacred. The word the Druid means 'man of oak'.

Ideograms and Mnemonics

The letters of the alphabet do not only function as speech signs or phonograms, they also act as ideograms or idea signs that convey more complex information, mainly religious and scientific (metaphysics). To assist in the recall of either of these functions, the letters were given mnemonic names, A – Alpha, etc., to act as memory aids for the teaching and learning of these functions.

A mystical interpretation of the meaning of the letters of the alphabet has been passed down through the ages as ideographic symbolism; magic signs that indicate a larger context or deeper meaning. In the case of the letters of the alphabets, the divine shape of the letter is its physical manifestation, a sort of portrait of its thematic character.

A simple example of letter symbolism is revealed in the first letter of a word which tells us the nature of the word, sometimes by the shape alone. In Mountain, the M has peaks and a valley. The hills on both sides of the V form the Valley. The H is a ladder, a Hill is easier to climb than a Mountain with its steep sides. Bumpy, the B is made of two bumps. Sudden, the S makes an abrupt change in direction. The T of Tree has a central trunk and outstretched branches. The Z makes a zigzag form.

The symbolism of letters varies according to each alphabet. The vowels and consonants of an occult alphabet perform different functions with pictorial and geometric interpretations. The vowels are round and sacred, they represent the visible planets and belong to God and are not to be written. The consonants are square and common, they represent the elements and constellations and belong to man.

In Mesopotamian sources, the letter A – Aleph, was originally a pictogram of an ox head; the Phoenicians turned it on its side, which implied a plough; the Greeks turned it upside down to express the notion of man with two feet firmly on the ground. The letter S was used by the Minoans to represent a snake, an image still suggested by the curve of the modern letter S.

The main pictographic source of letters is essentially Egypto-Canaanite: D – Daleth for tent flap or door; Y – Yod, meaning a prop; H – Cheth, meaning ploughed field; M – Mem, meaning water; P – Resh, meaning head; and O – Ayin, meaning eye.

The abstract heritage of letters is easier to see in the geometric Greco-Roman letters than the more cursive Hebrew and Arabic scripts, altered in shape over time by calligraphy.

In addition to the pictorial symbolism inherited from the ancients, the Greek mathematician, Pythagoras, reinvigorated the alphabet's geometric and mathematical symbolism. A letter's geometric symbolism is considered from every aspect. Some letters are older than others. These include prehistoric shapes directly identical to the early forms of the alphabetic letters DEZHOPSX, while G and J are recent. Most capital letters, ABEFHKLMNRSTVXYZ, are constructed in such a way as to portray the idea that they are reflections, a light and dark twin, a mirror image. C and D are the same upturned. O and I remain identical.

The letter's upper half is the mind, thought, spiritual plane; the lower half the material, physical, earth plane. A letter that is the same inverted – HNOSX – is active on both planes. This brings out the double strength of the letter. A letter that becomes a different letter when inverted is said to be duel. M has its feet firmly planted on the ground, so M is well organized and stable. But inverted it is W, reaching up for spiritual help in times of emotional upheaval.

The letter N is open, above and below, it is considered versatile and encounters many changes in life. The letters B and D are examples of closed letters, while C, E, F and G are examples of open letters.

The letter S is made up of two C's. The top being open to the spiritual plane; the bottom being open to the material plane. It can see into both worlds, revealing the fact that it has the wisdom of the serpent. It will snake between the two worlds before having to choose one.

Geometrically, the letter P is a circle on a line, representing the head of the self. The letter Y represents the crossroads of decision or a forking of the ways. The letter Q has a circle representing the spiritual sun, the line is the rod of balance. The vertical line of the letter I depicts spirit descending into matter, and vice versa.

The letter E is open to the future and doesn't look back. It is well balanced between the spiritual and physical worlds because the middle line is centered. The letter F is not as well balanced as the letter E and is therefore seen to 'carry the load'. The letters X and Y represent man in his extremities.

Ox/Plough - source of generation.
Air - first breath - diaphragm.
The diagonal lines give a balance of forces or energies. The central dividing line gives balance between the upper spiritual world and the lower material world. It is a picture of a man standing well balanced on two feet.

House, birth place, womb.
The nourishing Breast. Balls, Bollocks. A division between spirit and matter. A straight line down from the spirit becoming manifest in the physical - to 'be'.

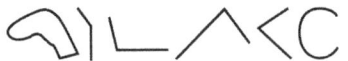

Camel, laden with riches, eloquent. An open mouth. A half moon giving light to the Earth.

Triangle. Door. Womb.
To go in or out. Life or Death. An upright line attached to a half moon. A letter of balance with self made boundaries.

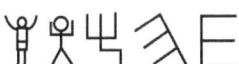

Open hand. Progression
Well balanced. Open to the future.

Unbalanced. Carries the load. Two outstretched arms to those near them.

Camel, laden with riches, eloquent. Turns in on itself. Open mouth but not as talkative as C.

Cultivated field. Consciousness. Window. Eye.

Pictographic and geometric symbolism of letter forms

Flame - the centre of light.
The vertical line depicts the spirit descending into matter so that man became a living soul.

Fish hook. New level of consciousness. Facing the past it retains memory in its cup of the hook.

Palm of hand. Holding.
Feet firmly on the ground, it holds its arm up and gives light, scattering its energies.

Ox goad. The outstretched arm of God in the act of accomplishment. A firm baseline balanced on the Earth.

Water. WoMb. WoMan. Mother. Mere. Strength of character, standing on its own two feet. Open to higher ideals.

Fish. Spiritual growth.
Well-balanced on the Earth plane, it has a dividing line between two worlds. It is open above and below.

Eye, inner eye, all-seeing eye of God. The Cosmos. Zero. All or nothing.

Mouth. Power of speech.
A circle on a line, the head on the self. Looking to the future.

Back of the head. Balance.
Mirth. The circle is the spiritual sun, the line is the rod of balance. The head with a tongue protruding.

Head. The Pineal gland.
The vertical line is upright man with a forward facing head, and one leg moving forward. A seeker of higher understanding.

Tooth, of fire, Flame. The "I AM" of Christ. Choice of paths. Made of two C's, one open to the spiritual, one to the material. Serpentine.

Cross. Self-sacrifice. Load on shoulders. Cross bar symbolises a roof, meaning protection, listening to ones inner self.

C scatters, L gathers, U is receptive. Normal way up, a cup or receptacle. Upside down, protection.

Peg. Nail. Eye. Thought.
Open above implies intelligence with no dividing line between the spiritual and the material.

The valleys and peaks denote change. Separation between being and non-being.

Bow used to shoot an arrow. Stands strong on the Earth plane, open to materialism. Its up-stretched arms inviting spiritual guidance.

Flame. A path with forked roads. Adolescence. Decisions.
Right path - Divine Wisdom.
Left path - Earthly Wisdom.

Weapon. Sword. Electricity. Energy. The diagonal line goes directly from spiritual to material, a direct line of current.

Chaldean Cabala

Chaldea is the ancient Greek name for the southern kingdom of Babylon, previously known as Sumer. The term 'Chaldean' is used to describe a system of ancient Middle Eastern magic that infuses imported Indic-Brahmi religious beliefs and elements of Persian Zoroastrianism, mixing them with native Sumerian-Babylonian mysticism.

Said to be lost to mankind, it is considered the more ancient system, possibly the root of all cabalistic wisdom, although Arabic scholars claim that some Chaldean works have been translated and preserved by some Sufic initiates.

Chaldean occult expertise lay in astrology and numerology, which they combined to divine the numerical values of a person's name and birth date. The belief in the magic power of the names of the deity also seems to have originated in Chaldea.

Sumerian/Chaldean deities were assigned with numbers. The most important deities were assigned with numbers that were mathematically important or useful. The mathematical properties of the numbers were reflected in the personalities of the deities assigned to the numbers. Each god was assigned to a planet or weather phenomenon and numbers with a strange musicality to them. The high gods were assigned regular numbers that divide the powers of 60, the basis of time keeping: 60 seconds, 60 minutes, etc. The use of regular numbers is common other ancient cultures, from the Sumerian sexagesimal system, to the Mayan Long Count Calendar and the Yuga's of Hinduism.

The fundamental difference between Chaldean and other cabalistic systems is the way the number values are designated. All other cabalistic systems designate number values according to the letter sequence of the alphabet, whereas Chaldean cabala designates the number values by sound vibration.

The Chaldean system does not assign the number 9 with a letter value because it is the most sacred of the numbers. Its vibratory force includes the attributes of all other numbers and therefore could not be represented by any individual letter. Because the number value system only goes up to 8, some consider it to be a more accurate system. This notion has its dissenters, who claim it is a modern invention more suited to a cabalistic expression of the English alphabet.

In astrology, the Chaldeans used an Earth-centered system (Earth, Moon, Mercury, Venus, Sun, Mars, Jupiter, Saturn) as they assumed that the planets that moved the fastest were closest to the Earth.

In Chaldean cosmology, the "unknown ideal deity" or "Ain Soph", held the highest plane in their mythology. Under Ain Soph were the seven planets in their seven orbits, or sphere's; the probable germ for the idea of the sephiroth. In Jewish cosmology, Iggulim or circles depict the ten sephiroth as smaller, concentric circles radiating inwards from the Divine Omnipresence.

Asomtavruli is an ancient, almost forgotten script native to the country of Georgia, situated north of Turkey in the Caucasus, a mountainous region that divides Europe from Asia. The Georgians believe they are descended from the Sumerians.

In 2002, two prominent Georgian scholars, Zurab Kapiandze and Teimuraz Mibchvani, claimed to have rediscovered the secrets of a magic system in the long forgotten Asomtavruli script. They arrived at this conclusion through years of painstaking research, correlating the signs from Sumerian artefacts, clay tablets and pottery, and signs that revealed over 200 lexical units of Sumerian-Georgian origin.

Asomtavruli contains 35 letters, the same number as contained in the first alphabet given by God to Adam. The letter forms are derived from a geometric pattern, a cosmogram or schema, called a Bakila in Georgian, the pattern of which is used in a children's game and found on small folded cakes called Bokhuana. With the addition of circles, this pattern reveals all the Asomtavruli letter forms.

According to the Georgian scholars, Asomtavruli is an alphabet of deities that describe the Sumerian version of the creation of the universe. It begins when the Earth was still covered in water and there was no land. The alphabet also functions as a calendar, its 35 letters form a numerical basis of 5 x 7 which works out to 360 days of the lunar calendar and reveals the date of the beginning of the first Sumerian civilization, 6504 BC; the date of the flood, 5700 BC; and the date of the post-deluvian Sumer beginning in 5604 BC. The scholars claim there is still much more to be discovered in Asomtavruli but whether the script turns out to be the long-lost original Sumerian linear alphabet is yet to be resolved.

Planets	Deities	Female Deiries
Heaven	60 - Anu	55 - Antu
Saturn	50 - Enlil	45 - Ninlil
Neptune	40 - Enki	35 - Ninki
Moon	30 - Sin	25 - Ningal
Sun	20 - Shamash	15 - Inana
Mars	10 - Adad	05 - Ninhursag

Chaldean deity corespondences

1	2	3	4	5	6	7	8
A	B	C	D	E	U	O	F
I	K	G	M	H	V	Z	P
J	R	L	T	N	W		
Q		S		X			
Y							

Chaldean numerology

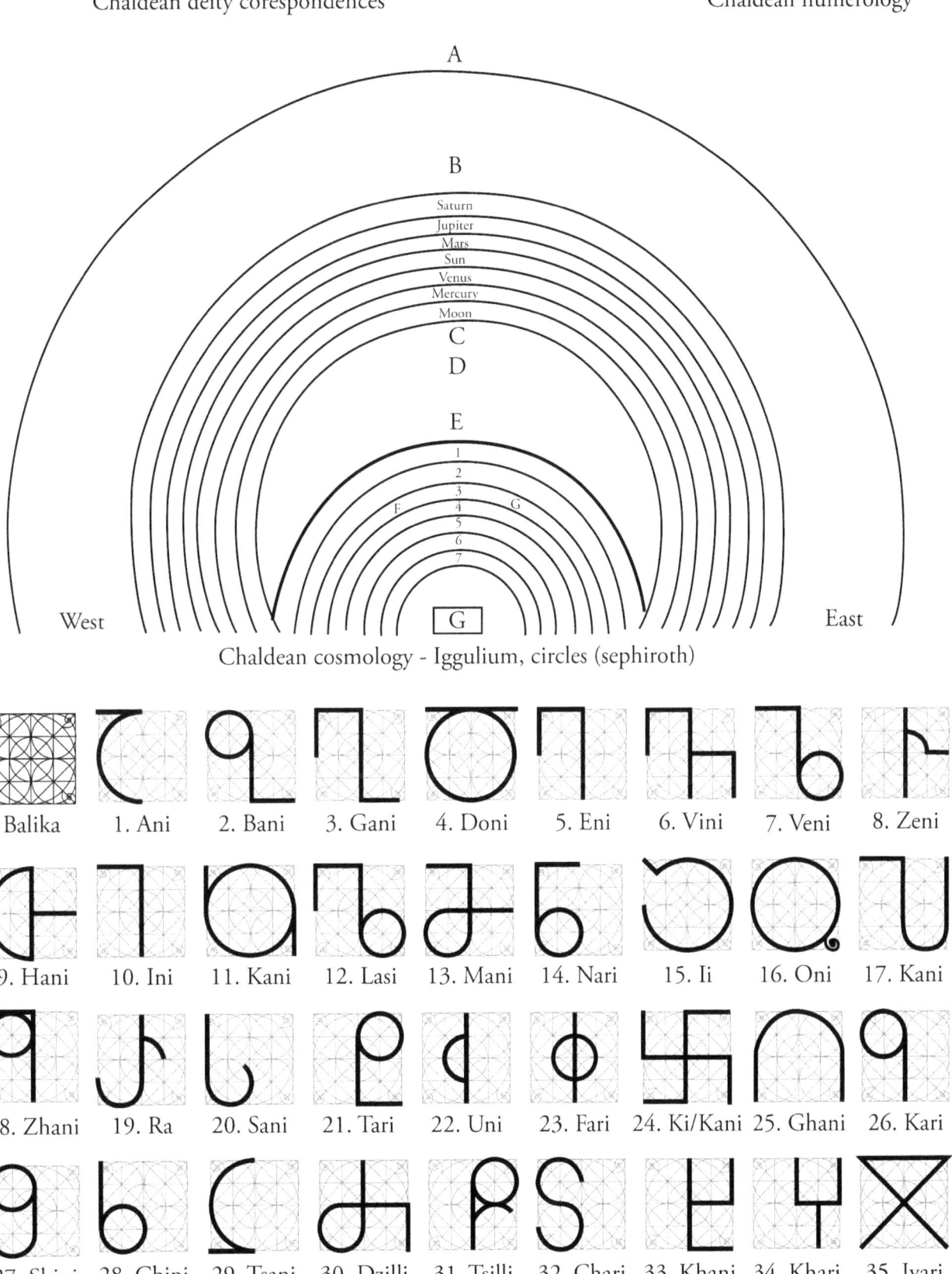

Chaldean cosmology - Iggulium, circles (sephiroth)

Balika, 1. Ani, 2. Bani, 3. Gani, 4. Doni, 5. Eni, 6. Vini, 7. Veni, 8. Zeni, 9. Hani, 10. Ini, 11. Kani, 12. Lasi, 13. Mani, 14. Nari, 15. Ii, 16. Oni, 17. Kani, 18. Zhani, 19. Ra, 20. Sani, 21. Tari, 22. Uni, 23. Fari, 24. Ki/Kani, 25. Ghani, 26. Kari, 27. Shini, 28. Chini, 29. Tsani, 30. Dzilli, 31. Tsilli, 32. Chari, 33. Khani, 34. Khari, 35. Jvari

Asomtavruli

Greek Cabala

For centuries, Greek cabala was thought to be a later development of Jewish cabala. It is now considered to be the origin of Gematria or Jewish number mysticism. Greek number mysticism or isosephy was first developed by the Greek philosopher and mathematician, Pythagoras. The word 'isosephos' comes from the meaning iso-equal, psephes-pebble, since it was common practice for the Greeks to use patterns of pebbles or stones to learn arithmetic. Such pebbles were also called 'kalkuli', the origin of the word 'calculate'.

Isosephy generally consists of determining the numerical value of a word or group of letters and relating it to other words by means of this value. The Greeks also composed poetry in the form of distichs and epigrams in which isosephy was used to calculate the number of each line, with the same value for each line.

Greek alphabetic-numerals are said to have originated in the eastern Greek colony of Miletus, maybe as early as the 8th century BCE. In the 6th century BCE, Pythagoras developed this system as it contained three archaic letters, digamma = 6, qoppa = 90 and sampi = 900, which he used with the 24 letters of the classical Greek alphabet, to give 27 letters in all. Enough symbols to represent the ordinal and cardinal number systems of 9 integers, 9 multiples of 10 and 9 multiples of 100.

The innovative idea of using letters to denote numbers was carried across the Mediterranean and Middle East during Alexander the Great's conquest of the Egyptians, Jews, Babylonians and Persians; all of whom eventually adopted the Greek system of using letters as numbers. The system continued in use through the Roman period into the Byzantine age, when they were replaced by Arabic numerals

Pythagoras was born in 582 BCE. The son of a stone-cutter, he studied at the Temple of the Melchizedek, where Jesus is said to have studied 600 years later. Learned in Greek philosophy, he was tutored by the Egyptian priests of Isis in Thebes and studied the mysteries of Adonis in Phoenicia and Syria. Jewish Rabbis taught him the secret traditions of Moses, and he was initiated into the Babylonian and Chaldean mysteries, where it is said he studied with Zoroaster. Further east, he studied in Hindustan with Brahmin priests.

Pythagoras is the first recorded figure in history to elevate numbers into the sphere of philosophy. He studied the connection between music and numbers and developed the idea that numbers were the key to the nature of the universe.

In 536 BCE, Pythagoras established the first 'academy' in history. The students received what Pythagoras considered the triangular foundation of all arts: occult mathematics, music and astronomy. Since number was the underlying principle of all three sciences, the science of numbers was considered to be the origin of all things. Here among esoteric lessons, the secrets of number vibration were given to a select few.

Pythagoras also studied music; he invented the seven-tone scale we use today. In doing this, he was able to add an eighth string to the seven stringed lyre of Apollo, allowing musicians more variety to play various modes of eight.

Pythagoras also noticed that the further from Earth the other planets were, the faster they moved. The friction caused by their movement produced various tones which he related to the mathematical principles of the musical scale. Concluding that the planets sing, creating the 'music of the spheres' which sounds like silence to the ear. This system was based on the secret doctrines of Orpheus, the patron of music, son of Apollo, god of music.

Pythagoras also invented a wheel of letters with numbers and astrological signs on it that encircled a globe. By using the number of the inquirer's name or birth date, it was possible to foretell future events. He died aged 75 in 507 BCE, murdered by an embittered student, and the school eventually closed.

Pythagorean doctrines formed the basis of Platonism in the first century CE; together they flourished as Neoplatonism in the 3rd century, using Pythagorean isosephy and the Platonic geometry of letter shapes to illustrate their philosophical concepts, stressing shape among the various qualities or attributes of letters. They believed that when God created order out of chaos 'all things were without proportion or measure,' i.e. in chaos. So God's first step was to 'set about reducing the elements of chaos to order by giving them a definite pattern of shape and number.'

Oridnal	Cardinal	Name	Sound	Capital	Ancient Letter	Meaning
1	1	Alpha	A	Α		cattle
2	2	Beta	B,	Β		demon
3	3	Gamma	G	Γ		divinity
4	4	Delta	D	Δ		fourfold
5	5	Epsilon	E	Ε		ether
6	6	Diagamma	F		Ϝ ς	
7	7	Zeta	Z	Ζ		sacrifice
8	8	Eta	H	Η		joy
9	9	Theta	Th	Θ		crystal sphere
10	10	Iota	I,J,Y	Ι		destiny
11	20	Kappa	K	Κ		illness
12	30	Lambda	L	Λ		growth
13	40	Mu	M	Μ		trees
14	50	Nu	N	Ν		hag
15	60	Ksi	X/Ks	Ξ		fifteen stars
16	70	Omicron	O	Ο		sun
17	80	Pi	P	Π		solar halo
18	90	Qoppa	Q		ϛ ϙ	
19	100	Rho	R	Ρ		fruitfulness
20	200	Sigma	S	Σ		psychopomp
21	300	Tau	T	Τ		human being
22	400	Upsilon	U, Y	Υ		flow
23	500	Phi	Ph, F	Φ		phallus
24	600	Chi	Kh, X	Χ		property
25	700	Psi	Ps	Ψ		heavenly light
26	800	Omega	OO	Ω		abundance
27	900	San/Sampi	SS		⋔ Ɜ ⋌	

Letter values

1	2	3	4	5	6	7	8	9
Α	Β	Γ	Δ	Ε	ς	Ζ	Η	Θ
Ι	Κ	Λ	Μ	Ν	Ξ	Ο	Π	ϙ
Ρ	Σ	Τ	Υ	Φ	Χ	Ψ	Ω	⋌

Greek

1	2	3	4	5	6	7	8	9
A	B	C	D	E	F	G	H	I
J	K	L	M	N	O	P	Q	R
S	T	U	V	W	X	Y	Z	&

English

Isosephy/Gematria

Over the millennia, Greeks, Jews, Gnostics, Christians and Muslims have used isosephy (number-mysticism) and its various techniques to divine the secret name of God. Examples of the name of God can be revealed in many number values. For example, the Egyptian god Sarapis revealed his name to Alexander the Great using the numerical formula 200 1 100 1 80 10 200, which corresponds to the Greek word SARAPIS. Another example asserts the numerical equivalence between QEOS (Theos/God), HAGIOS (Hagios/Holy) and AGAQOS (Agathos/Good), as they all total 284.

The isosephic tradition of Gematria is commonly associated with the mystical Jewish alphabet, mainly due to the belief that the Torah, the Jewish Holy Book, is a cabalistic work. In such rabbinic literature, it is said that God revealed his name to the Israelites to be YHWH or Yahweh (Jehovah). In Hebrew mysticism, this Divine Tetragram is the only true name of God. When Gematria is applied to these letters, they total 26, the number of the name of God.

Gematria also allows for numerical correspondences. The two terms, Ekhad = One, and Ahavah = Love, correspond to the central concept that 'God is Love'. Individually, both words total 13; added together their sum is 26, the number of the name of God.

When the letters YHVH are written in a column on the page they can give an image of a person, who is given the name of Adam Cadmon. An androgynous being, both male and female, whose frequency is the light body of YYHVH

Gnosticism is a religious doctrine which appeared in the early centuries CE. To know the name of God was the spiritual aim of the Gnostics, who did not pretend to know the name of God but they believed it possible to learn its formula, this formula was the name of God.

The Gnostic God united in himself the 365 minor gods of the days of the year and as such his number was 365. The Gnostics made up the name 'Abrasax' whose letter values add up to 365. Though the name of God remained unknown, it was known that it had the character to be the ideal holy name. Therefore, 'Hagion Onoma' (Holy Name) became a name of God, not only for a metaphysical or religious reason but because it had the same number as Abrasax, 365.

Through the use of isosephy, the Gnostics divined other such discoveries. In ancient Egypt, the god Osiris was the God of the Year and their name for the river Nile. Nile spelt in Greek, Neilos, has the number 365. Again, the Greek spelling of Mithras (Miethras), the Persian Sun God, has the value 365. The letters of the magic word Abracadabra add up to 365, so it encompasses an entire year.

Not only did the Gnostics seek to find the true name of God in the number 365, they also sought it in the number 7. As from God proceeded the magical powers of the 7 vowels, 7 planets, 7 notes of the musical scale, 7 metals, and the 7 days of the week. The 7 vowels were a reflection of the Solar God's secret name, hidden in the days of the week – WAOUEIY or JIEVOAW

Just as the Gnostics drew miraculous consequences from the practice of isosephy and were preoccupied with the quest to know the name of God, which adds up to 365, Christian mystics speculated on the number 666. 666 is the number given by the Apostle John to the 'Beast of the Apocalypse', a monster identified as the Antichrist.

The isosephic value of 666 is an obvious one, but the system to be used was not stated, leading to many attempts using different systems. Taking 666 to be 'the number of a man', the names of historical figures have been calculated for answers. Nero, the first Roman Emperor to persecute the Christians, has been identified as the Beast of the Apocalypse, since the number of his name accompanied by the title Caesar totals 666 using the Hebraic system.

On the same lines, the name of another Roman Emperor, Diocletian Augustus, who violently persecuted Christians, totals 666 when using Roman numerals. Others who interpreted 666 to mean the number of a 'type of man' calculated the Greek word Lateinos, meaning Latins or Romans, to be 666.

Much later in time, a Catholic mystic claimed to demonstrate that the German reformer Luther was the Antichrist, as his name gives the number 666. Lutherans, who considered the Church of Rome to be the direct heir of the Empire of the Caesars, responded by taking the Roman numerals contained in the phrase VICARUS FILII DEI, 'Vicar of the Son of God', inscribed on the Papal Tiara, to total 666.

H	V	H	Y
5	6	5	10 = 26

Yod
He
Vau
He

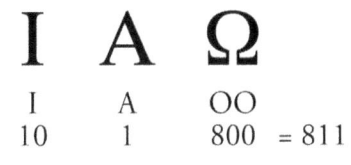

I	A	Ω
I	A	OO
10	1	800 = 811

Alpha and Omega - Jesus Christ

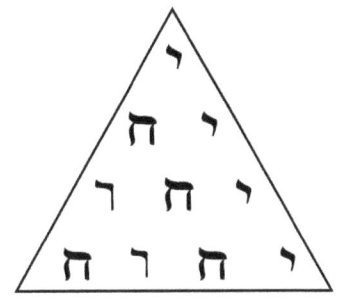

26 = YHWH - Divine Tetragram

YHVH - Adam Kadmon
Divine Names

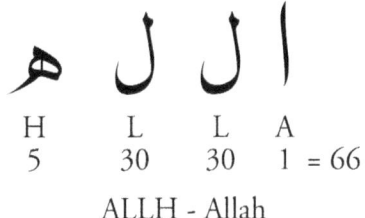

H	L	L	A
5	30	30	1 = 66

ALLH - Allah

A B R A S A X
1 2 100 1 200 1 60 = 365

Abrasax

A G I O N   O N O M A
1 3 10 70 50   70 50 70 40 1 = 365

Hagion Onona - Holy Name

N E I L O S
50 5 10 30 70 200 = 365

Neillos - Nile (Osiris)

M E I Q R A S
40 5 10 9 100 1 200 = 365

Mithras - Persian Sun God

365 = Sacred names of the God of the Year

N	V	R	N	R	S	Q
50	6	200	50	200	60	100 = 666

QSAR NERO - Hebrew - Ceaser Nero as the Devil - 666

DIoCLes aVgVstVs
500 1 100 50   5   5   5 = 666

Roman numerals - Diocletian Augustus as the number of the beast

LATEINOS
30 1 300 5 10 50 70 200 = 666

Lateinos - Latins

LVTHERNVC
30 200 100 8 5 80 40 200 3 = 666

(Martin) Luther

VICarIVs fILII DeI
5 1 100   1 5   1 50 1 1 500   1 = 666

Vicar of the Son of God (Papal Tiara)

666 - the Number of the Beast

Correspondence

The connection between the stars and the letters of the alphabet is very old. Early observers of the heavens noted that there were two distinct groups of stars; the 'fixed' stars or constellations and the 'wandering' stars or planets (Gk. planetes – wanderer). The five planets that are visible to the naked eye are Mercury, Venus, Mars, Jupiter and Saturn. Together with the Sun and the Moon, the planets total seven. Of the 24 letters of the Greek alphabet, the seven vowels were allocated to the planets, five consonants to the elements and the remaining twelve consonants to the twelve constellations of the zodiac. This set of Greek alphabetical attributes are somewhat similar to the Hebrew alphabet in the Sefer Yetzirah.

In Greek mysticism, Aristotle refers to the fact that the vowels and consonants of the Greek alphabet had various sets of symbolic correspondences attached to them. The Greeks received their knowledge of the planets from the older civilizations of Egypt and Babylon. This knowledge included the association of the planets with individual gods – a practice that is still preserved in the names of Greco-Roman deities given to the planets, and the names of Germanic deities for the days of the week.

By employing number mysticism, the seven planets were quickly associated with the seven vowels of the Greek alphabet, and the vowels came to represent the powers of the planetary gods. In later Christian mysticism, the planets were replaced by the Archangels.

The numerical association of seven planets to seven vowels revealed the order of the vowels to be representative of the Greek model of the planetary order of the solar system with Earth at the center. From Earth, the order of the planets proceeds as follows: Moon, Mercury, Venus, Sun, Mars, Jupiter and Saturn. This gave a magical sequence or formula to the Greek vowel order.

According to the Pythagorean Mysteries, the distances and speeds of the planets' orbits created a harmony known as 'the music of the spheres' that sounds like silence to the human ear. Because the planets created the music of the spheres, both the planets and the notes of the musical scale were associated with the seven vowels. This led to invocations stating, "In your seven-letter name is established the harmony of the seven sounds." The sequence A E H I O Y W became known as the elements or 'stoichea' (to move in a row), since they represented the seven planets or elements of the cosmos and their musical notes.

The symbolic correspondence of the number seven was extended to include not only number, sound, symbol, note, planet, god and day, but other correspondences including the Pleiades and Ursa Major star groups, spiritual heavens, angels, body parts, gems, metals, flowers, herbs, colours, emotions, virtues, vices and incenses. As the mystic signs of the planets, the 7 vowels are repeated in many spells and charms. They were called 'the seven deathless gods' or 'the seven letters of the magician'.

The mystical connection between letters and the heavens was extended to the remaining 17 consonants of the Greek alphabet. Five of the consonants were allocated to the five elements and the remaining twelve to the constellations of the zodiac. Like the planets, they formed the basis for a wide range of correspondences.

The consonants became part of these when it was noted that the Greek words for the elements used only five consonants between them, GPDQR, the rest of the letters being vowels. The elements were denoted acrophonically, being represented by the initial letter of their name. GH (Ge – earth), PYR (pyr – fire), UDWR (hydor – water), AIQHR (aither – ether), AHR (aer – air). These consonants would logically equate to their Aristotelian attributes.

The remaining 12 consonants were allocated to the 12 constellations of the zodiac. The numerous correspondences attached to the signs of the zodiac meant they could be divided into different groups. Each individual sign of the zodiac being ruled by either air, fire, water or earth, they could be grouped according to element. In another zodiacal system, the 24 Greek letters were allocated to the 12 signs of the zodiac in pairs. This formed the basis for a system known as Onomatic astrology, in which the zodiacal attribute of each letter of the name of the party concerned could be converted into a pseudo-astrological chart.

Letter	Sound	Planet	Greek god	Day	Note	Scale	Metal	Archangel	Colour	Direction
A	A	Moon	Hecate	Monday	A	si	silver	Michael	violet	East
E	E	Mercury	Hermes	Wednesday	E	mi	mercury	Gabriel	yellow	North
H	EE	Venus	Aphrodite	Friday	B	la	copper	Raphael	indigo	West
I	I	Sun	Apollo	Sunday	D	re	gold	Suriel	orange	South
O	O	Mars	Ares	Tuesday	C	do	iron	Raguel	red	Down
U	U	Jupiter	Zeus	Thurday	G	sol	tin	Anael	blue	Up
W	OU	Saturn	Kronos	Saturday	F	fa	lead	Saraphael	green	Centre

7 Greek vowels and their correspondences

Letter	Element	Qualities	Greek god	Platonic solid
G	Earth	cold and dry	Hades	cube
D	Water	cold and wet	Chronos	icosahedron
Q	Ether	all	Zeus	dodecahedron
P	Fire	hot and dry	Ares	tetrahedon
R	Air	hot and wet	Dionysus	octahedron

5 Greek consonants, their elements and correspondences

Letter	Zodiac sign	Month
B	Aries	March / April
Z	Taurus	April / May
K	Gemini	May / June
L	Cancer	June / July
M	Leo	July / August
N	Virgo	August / September
X	Libra	September / October
S	Scorpio	October / November
T	Sagitarius	November / December
F	Capricorn	December / January
C	Aquarius	January / February
Y	Pisces	February / March

12 Greek consonants and the signs of the zodiac and the months of the year

א	air	ל	Libra
ב	MERCURY	מ ם	water
ג	MOON	נ	Scorpio
ד	VENUS	ס	Sagitarius
ה	Aries	ע	Capricorn
ו	Taurus	פ ף	MARS
ז	Gemini	צ ץ	Aries
ח	Cancer	ק	Pisces
ט	Leo	ר	SUN
י	Virgo	ש	fire
כ	JUPITER	ת	SATURN

22 letters of the Hebrew alphabet of Sephirothic Order of the Golden Dawn

Jewish Cabala

Early initiates of the cabalistic mysteries believed its principles were first taught by God to a school of angels before the Fall of man. The angels later communicated the secrets to Adam, so that humanity might regain its lost estate. Different angels were employed to initiate the succeeding Patriarchs in the cabalistic mysteries. In the Old Testament narrative, cabala is passed on from Adam through to Enoch, down to Noah and on to Abraham, from Abraham to his son Isaac, thence to Jacob and so on. Moses was initiated into the cabalistic mysteries by God on Mount Sinai, where God gave him a sacred rendering of the laws that the Israelites should observe. Moses then concealed the secret instructions of God in the first four books of the Pentateuch.

In 332 BCE, Alexander the Great conquered Judea. The lingua franca of his empire was 'koine' or common Greek, and the Jews were forced to administer their country using the Greek alpha-numerical writing system. During the conquests of Alexander, a great mingling of esoteric knowledge took place in the Ptolemaic Egyptian capital of Alexandria. It was at Alexandria that the most important books of Jewish mysticism were translated into Greek. At the time of Alexander, there were more Jews living in Alexandria than there were in Jerusalem and the translation of Jewish Holy Books into Greek was the watershed in the wider development of cabala.

Over the next 600 years, various secret doctrines diverged into numerous sects and schools, mixing Chaldean, Babylonian, Egyptian, Hebrew, Greek, Gnostic, Christian and Sufic mysteries. It is amongst these teaching that the origins of Jewish cabala can be traced, a mixing of Hebrew mysticism and Greek Neoplatonism.

In 13th century Europe, Jewish cabala emerged suddenly in France and Spain. Its doctrines are found in books such as the Sefer Ha Zohar, the Sefer Ha Yetzirah and other literature of Hebrew mysticism, linking them to an earlier tradition by references to those texts. This had a huge influence on the Western magical tradition, which relied heavily on Jewish esoteric lore as a source for the inner gnosis of orthodox Christian thought.

In Jewish cabala, there are three main techniques of isosephy for calculating letters, they are: Gematria, a method of figuring hidden meanings from the geometric shape of letters and from the numerical values of both words and phrases; Temurah, the art of finding words within words and from anagrams; and Notariqon, which derives words from abbreviations and the initials of words.

Gematria is one of the most widely known cabalistic techniques. Each letter has a number value. For instance, 'aleph', the first letter of the alphabet, is number 1. By adding up the value of each letter in a word, a numerical value is obtained for the whole word. For example, the word ALPh (aleph), the spelling of the first letter of the Hebrew alphabet, totals 111 (A=1+L=30+Ph=80). The Hebrew phrase AChD HVA ALHYM (Achad ho Elohim) translates as 'He is one God' and also totals 111 (A=1+Ch=8+D=4+H=5+V=6+A=1+A=1+L=30+H=5+Y=10+M=40). In this manner, Gematria establishes a link between seemingly unrelated ideas.

Temurah is a complex system in which tables of combinations are established and new words are formed by replacing each letter of a word with its 'mate' letter. It uses 'root' meanings of words to form links within words from that root. Notariquon shows how each letter of a word can serve as a first initial for another word. The prologue of the Zohar provides an example of this. There is a tale about how each letter appeared in turn before God, asking that it serve as the start of creation (i.e. the first letter of the first word of the Torah). Before 'Beth' is chosen, the other letters parade before God and explain why they should be so honoured, and God explains his reasons for rejecting their pleas. Throughout this process, initials play a prominent role. Consider one example: the letter 'Ayin'. Favouring 'Ayin' was the fact that it is the first letter of the word 'modesty' (AyNVH; anovo). But 'Ayin' was rejected because it is also the first letter of the word for 'iniquity' (AyVl; auvel).

Notariquon, is a less well-known technique. One Hebrew word can serve as a set of initials for a phrase where each letter of a word is regarded as the first initial of a completely separate word. BRAShYTh (in the beginning) is the first word of the Torah, the Jewish holy book. Assuming each of those letters represents the beginning of a separate word, it can be expanded into the following: BrAShYTh RAH ALHYM ShYQBLV YShRAL TVRH, which translates as "In the beginning, God saw that Israel would accept the Torah."

Number Value	Hebrew Letter	Letter Sound	Hebrew Name	Name Meaning	Tarot Card Equivalent
1/100	א	A	Aleph	ox	Fool
2	ב	B	Beth	house	Magian
3	ג	G	Gimmel	camel	Empress
4	ד	D	Daleth	door	Emperor
5	ה	H	He	window	Heirophant
6	ו	V/W	Vau/Waw	hook	Lovers
7	ז	Z	Zayin	sword	
8	ח	Ch	Cheth	fence	Chariot
9	ט	Th	Teth	serpent	Strength
10	י	Y/I/J	Yod	hand	Hermit
20/500	כ	K	Kaph	palm of hand	Wheel of Fortune
30	ל	L	Lamed	ox goad	Justice
40/600	מ	M	Mem	water	Hanged Man
50/700	נ	N	Nun	fish	Death
60	ס	X/SS	Samekh	support	Temperence
70	ע	O	Ayin	eye	Devil
80/800	פ	P	Pe	mouth	Tower
90/900	צ	Tz	Tzaddi	fish hook	Star
100	ק	Q	Qoph	back of head	Moon
200	ר	R	Resh	head	Sun
300	ש	Sh	Shin	tooth-flame	Judgement
400	ת	T	Tau	sign	World

Letter values

1	2	3	4	5	6	7	8	9
א	ב	ג	ד	ה	ו	ז	ח	ט
י	כ	ל	מ	נ	ס	ע	פ	צ
ק	ר	ש	ת	ן	ם	ף	ץ	

Number system

Celestial Alphabet

According to Jewish cabala, God conceived the letters of the alphabet to create the Cosmos according to His Will. In His Earthly realm, man uses the alphabet to create reality according to his will, as a tool used to exercise control over those events that humans do not have direct control over. This requires detailed knowledge of the esoteric, of the self and of cosmology, which is to be found in the mysticism of cabala.

This heavily edited version of the Celestial Alphabet is taken from the Serfira Ha Zohar or Book of Splendor. It relates the story of how God ordered the letters of the alphabet at the moment of Creation.

'One by one the letters made their case to the Divine Presence on why he should create the world by them. The Divine Presence listened to their pleas before giving his reasons why each letter would not be chosen, returning them to their previous position in the alphabet, until only B (Beth) and A (Aleph) remained.

Beth moved forward to make his case and said: "Create the world by me, because I am the initial letter of Beracha (blessing) and through me all will bless thee, both in the world above as in the world below." "Truly Beth," said the holy one, "I will surely create the world by thee only."

Hearing these words, Aleph remained in its place and went not to the Divine Presence, who therefore exclaimed, "Aleph, Aleph! Why commest thou not before me as all the other letters?" Aleph replied: "Lord and sovereign of the universe, it is because I have observed that, except for Beth, they have all returned as they went, without success."

To these words the Holy One responded: "Aleph, Aleph! Thou shalt be the first of all letters and my unity shall be symbolized only by thee. In all conceptions and ideas, human or divine, in every act and deed begun, carried and completed, in all of them shalt thou be the first, the beginning."

Therefore, the Book of Genesis begins with two words whose initials are B: Berashith Bara (in the beginning created) followed by two others, whose initials are A: Alhim ath (God, the substance of) to show that the letters of these alphabets celestial and earthly are one and the same by which every creature and thing in the universe has been formed and produced.'

Another Jewish cabalistic work, Sephira Ha Yetzirah or the Book of Foundation, reveals how God is said to facilitate the creation by using elements of Himself in the form of the letters of the alphabet. From His Holy Spirit, He created A, and from A sprang Air, and in Air He formed the remaining 21 letters of the Hebrew alphabet. This magic process is expressed in full by the Sefer Yetzirah or 'Double Star of Creation'.

In the Sefer Yetzirah, the central triangle contains a dot indicating God, the creative principle, surrounded by the 3 'mother' letters, representing the elements of air, fire and water. The spirit of God dwells within the center triangle, the Holy Temple that sustains all. From the center He created all there is by the three seraphim, numbers, letters and sounds, which are one and the same. The Voice, Spirit and Word of the Holy Spirit formed these three. They were called the mother letters because everything came from those basic elements.

The inner star holds the seven double-letters or vowels that symbolize all the good and bad that humans encounter in each life. Each letter is like a balance board with its good quality one side and its opposite extreme on the other; i.e. B – wisdom/foolishness, G – riches/poverty, D – fertility/sterility, Ch – life/death, P – power/servitude, R – peace/war, Th – beauty/deformity. Of these seven letters He formed the seven planets, seven days of the week, the seven notes on the musical scale, the seven colours of the rainbow and the seven openings for the senses: two eyes, two ears, two nostrils and one mouth.

The seven double-letters and the three mother letters combine to make the ten sephiroth which are His qualities and attributes. They are the ten emanations of number. The remaining 12 simple letters or consonants of the outer star represent the signs of the zodiac, the months of the year, the hours of the night and day and the major organs of the body.

By designating the weights, amounts and groupings of the 22 letters, God made all things. He placed the letters around a spherical wall with 231 doorways or gates. He turned the globe forward and backward to create good and evil, as all things must have a front and back.

The Sefer Yetzirah is also symbolic of the Sephirothic Tree. The triangle is symbolic of the three horizontal branches. The seven-pointed star symbolizes the seven vertical paths, and the twelve-pointed star indicates the twelve diagonal paths.

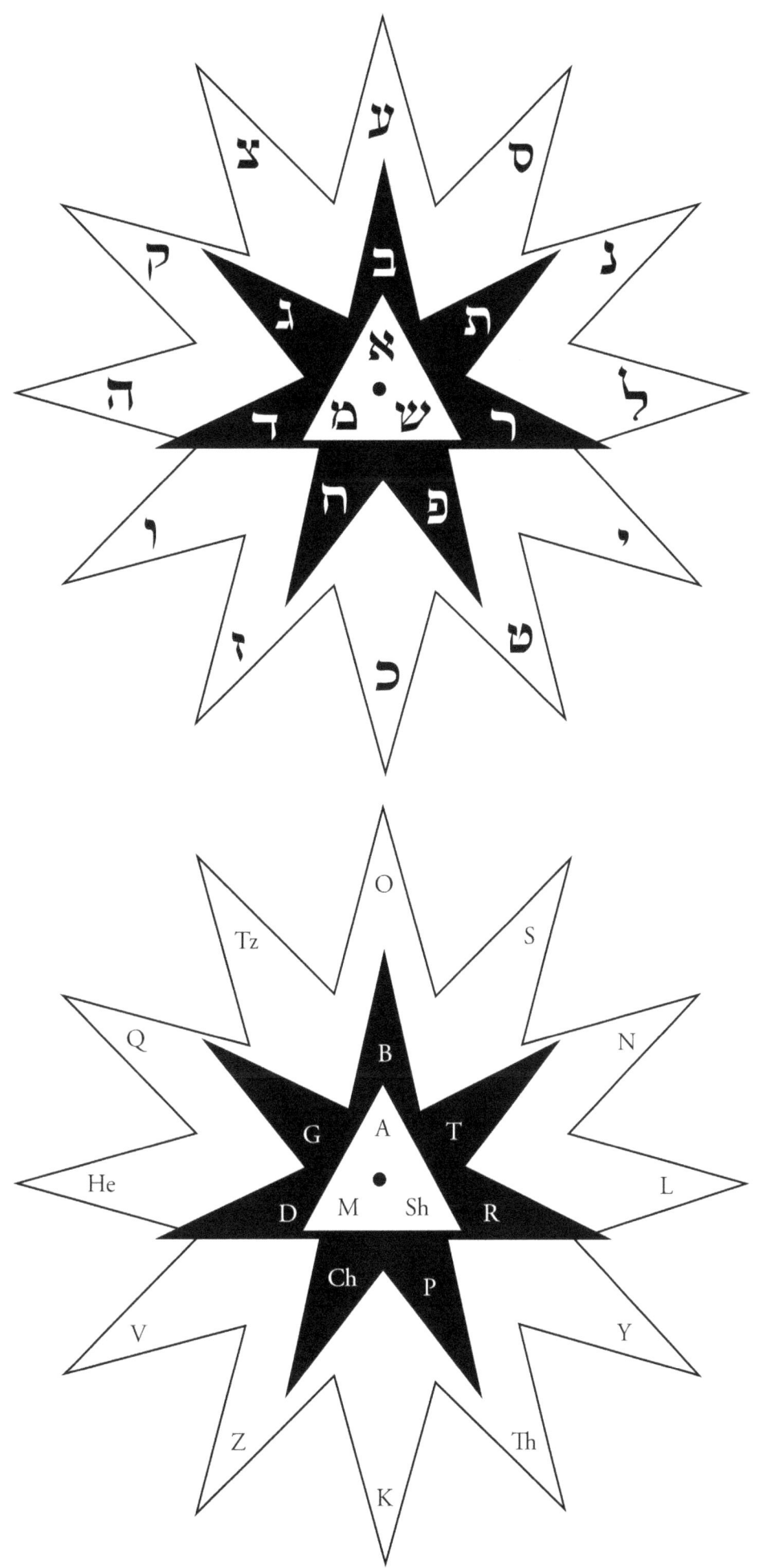

Double Star of the Sephir Yetzirah (Hebrew and English)

Sephirothic Tree

The Sephirothic Tree, Tree of Life, Cosmic Tree or Otz Chaiim in Hebrew, is a construct of the universe expressed by 10 spheres and their 22 connecting paths. The 10 spheres are called sephiroth, each has a name and they are numbered 1 to 10. They represent distinct attributes of the Creator.

The ten sephiroth are connected by 22 paths – three horizontal, seven vertical and twelve diagonal. They are represented by the 22 letters of the Hebrew alphabet and numbered 11 to 33, each with its own correspondences.

Together, the 10 sephiroth and 22 paths are known as the 32 Paths of Wisdom, the equivalent of the 32 degrees of Freemasonry and symbolize the entire universe or the body of God.

There are other connections between the sephiroth that are not associated with the letters, they are called "hidden" or "secret" paths, often marked in white.

Although predominately considered Jewish, the sephirothic system is universal and their order and relationship to numbers, planets and elements are thought to have their roots in Chaldean mysticism. During the Babylonian captivity, the Chaldean religious tradition was embraced by apostate Jews.

The disseminators of the Chaldean tradition in the few centuries before Christ were known as Taniam, the first cabalists among the Jews. They appeared in Jerusalem around 300 BCE with a secret doctrine identical to the Persian wisdom of Magic. Their knowledge was later developed into a written compendium of esoteric literature known as the Jewish cabala, delivered to subsequent generations by word of mouth. The first important Jewish cabalist was Jeshoshub ben Pandira, known to us as Jesus the Christ.

Among these practices are the rapid recitation of the Holy Name of God, YHVH or Tetrameter, meditations on the 10 sephiroth of the Tree of Life which is said to be emanations of God, learning to use the 22 letters of the Hebrew alphabet as a force carrying energy patterns which serve as the building blocks of the cosmos, and finally, transcending the space/time limitations of the physical world to realize one's inner divinity.

For about 500 years, the sephirothic system of the cabalistic Tree of Life has been the model of the universe in Western occultism. The traditional form, the Yosher or Upright Tree, is derived from Hermetic Christian and Jewish Neoplatonic mysticism.

In the Hebrew language, the words sephira – singular, and sephiroth – plural, are derived from the root word SPHR, which has many meanings linked to numbers and writing. In cabala, they are used to mean number, to number, to count, and to cipher; and cipher is the figure 0. It also means there is a hidden message containing its own key. SPHR is also the root of sephra or scribe.

Emanation theology is the basis for cabala and the foundations of cabala are the ten sephiroth – emanations or creative forces that stand for the manifestation of the universe in sound, number and letter, through which the Infinite (Ain Soph) reveals himself and continuously creates both the physical realm and the higher metaphysical levels.

The sephiroth are depicted as ten circles, spheres or globes of light that emanate from the Divine, who is represented by a dot or point in the center of each globe. Each globe contains a sephira or number, from 1 to 10, and each individual sphere also contains all numbers inside the ten, which is the cypher itself. The large cypher divided in half is the 1 and the 0.

The spheres also contain the sephira's correspondences or attributes (planetary ruler, divine name and angelic names), represented in three concentric circles. Each of the ten globes on the tree has its own particular name which shows the qualities and attributes of the Creator. The number is the vibrational rate of those qualities note and the letter is its signature or sign. These are the ingredients for all of creation

The first sephira is called Kether and the last Malkuth; there is an eleventh, invisible sphere called Daath which is not considered to be a sephira. The first three sephira (Kether, Binah, Chokmah), form the creative activities of the universe. The remaining seven sephiroth (Chesed, Geburah, Tiporeth, Netzach, Hod, Jesod, Malkuth), form the material world. The names of the sephira can be converted into geometric shapes called lineal figures. The number of letters in a name decides the shape of the figure. KTR = 3 – triangle, CCMH = 4 – square, MLKUT = 5 – pentagram, etc.

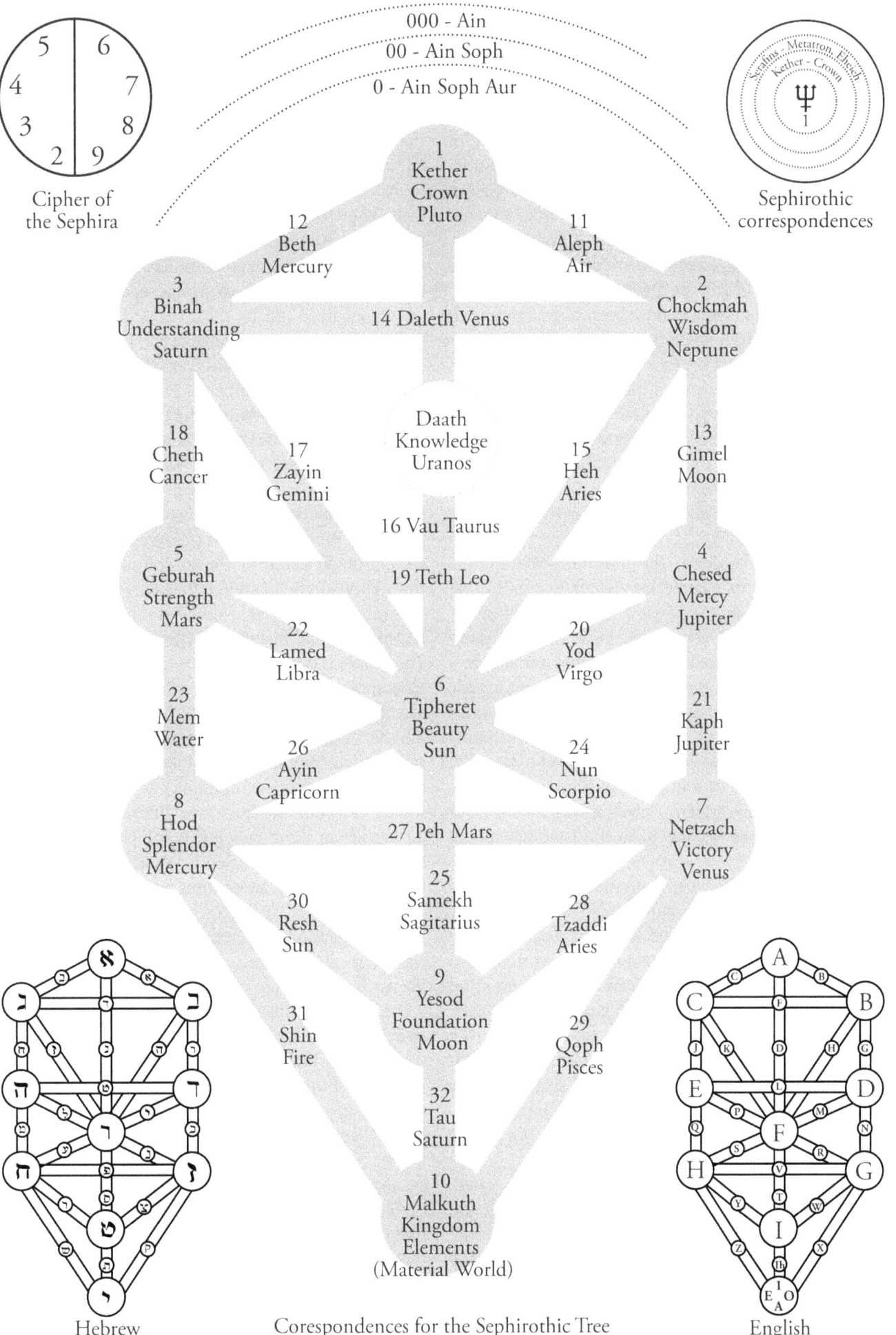

Corespondences for the Sephirothic Tree

Arabic Cabala

In 489 CE, Emperor Nero closed the Academy of Edessa in Syria and the center of ancient wisdom moved to the Persian Academy of Jundi Sabur. Henceforth, the advancement of the arts, sciences and medicines became the domain of Arabic culture. Arab mystics managed to preserve the classic works of the ancient world and the algebra of ancient India. In fact, cabala itself is said to have been started by an 8th century Sufic group known as The Faithful Brothers of Basra.

During the 10th century, previous works thought to be lost to Western civilization suddenly became available and influenced many greats of the Western magical tradition, the Knights Templar, Catholic theologians, the Troubadours, the Chivalric Round Table, the Rosicrucian's, Aleister Crowley and the Carboini of Italy.

In Arabic theology, the Prophet Muhammad was the maker of Islamic law which comes in two forms: Sharia and Tasawuf, also called Sufism. Sufism began in 7th century Persia as esoteric Islam. The metaphysical tradition states that Sufism is a continuation of the guidance of the ancient mystic science that goes back to Babylon and Hermes Trismegistus (Hermes the Thrice Great) who many believe was the first supreme adept who founded Western metaphysics, and that all schools from Sufism to the Neoplatonic system, Cabala and Gnosticism are his heirs. Hermes is equated to the Islamic Prophet Idries.

The early Sufis were mystics who practiced under the guidance of Muhammad and the major disciples. They studied the Tasawuf and set aside the literal meaning of Muhammad's words for a mystical interpretation. They later became influenced by Arabic Neoplatonism and Vendanta Hinduism. During the 8th century, Sufism spread across the Islamic empire due to a revival of Jewish mysticism. It then spread across the medieval world, from southern Europe to northern India and southern China. Traditional and fundamental Muslims do not accept Sufism as legitimate, to them it is a sin.

The Faithful Brothers were founded in Basra, Iraq, 950 CE. Strongly influenced by Aristotalism and Neoplatonism, their most influential work was the Rasa'il (letters), an encyclopedia containing all the alchemical, esoteric and metaphysical knowledge of the time. In 1160, their works were burnt in Baghdad by the orthodox Islamic church.

As the Sufis did, they too considered themselves to be the true heirs to the most ancient wisdom of Pythagoras and Hermes. Their writings are important as they summarize Arabian philosophy in the period prior to the mingling of Arabic and Western ideas which occurred during the 11th and 12th centuries. The Brethren had knowledge of the Tree of Life which featured only eight sephirot, a formula still used by Rosicrucian's. The number of sephirot was increased to ten by Jewish mystics during the 11th century.

By the 13th century, Sufic esoteric lore had begun to influence the West with its interpretations of Plato and Aristotle, giving it access to these ideas just as Europe was coming out of the so-called Dark Ages. The Renaissance and the Age of Enlightenment were brought about by the spread of Arabic wisdom through Moorish Spain into Europe.

Arabs call their alphabetic-numeral system Huruf Al Jamal, meaning 'totals by means of letters'. The system is modelled on the Hebrew one but also incorporates elements of the Greek system. The Hebrew order of the 22 letters represents the numbers under 400 and added 6 further conventional signs to accommodate the numbers from 400 to 1000, to achieve a system of numerals which was complete from 1 to 1000. There are two different systems used by Arabic-speaking peoples, in which the value of 6 letters differ. The first used by Middle Eastern Arabs; the second, a later adaptation used by North African Arabs.

Since each Arabic letter is the first letter of one of the attributes of Allah – Alif, the first letter of Allah; Ba, is the first letter of Baqi, 'He who remains', etc. – the use of Arabic letters led to the 'Most Secret' system. In this system, each letter is assigned not its usual value, but instead, the number of the Divine attribute of which it is the first letter. For instance, Alif, the first letter of Allah, whose usual value is 1, is given the number 66, which is the number of the name of Allah calculated according to the Abjad system. This is the system used in the symbolic theology called da'wa, 'invocation', which allows the forecasting and speculation of the past, present and the future, allowing magicians to contrive talismans and magic squares.

Number	Letter	Sound	Name	Name	Meaning	Number
1	ا	A	Alif	Allah	Allah	66
2	ب	B	Ba	Baqi	He who remains	113
3	ج	J	Jim	Jami	He who collects	114
4	د	D	Dal	Dayan	Judge	65
5	ه	H	Ha	Hadi	Guide	20
6	و	W	Wa	Wali	Master	46
7	ز	Z	Zay	Zaki	Purifier	37
8	ح	H	Ha	Haq	Truth	108
9	ط	T	Ta	Tahir	Saint	215
10	ي	Y	Ya	Yassin	Chief	130
20	ك	K	Kaf	Kafi	Sufficient	111
30	ل	L	Lam	Latif	Benevolent	129
40	م	M	Mim	Malik	King	90
50	ن	N	Nin	Nur	Light	256
60	س	S	Sin	Sami	Listener	180
70	ع	O	Ayin	Ali	Raised up	110
80	ف	F	Fa	Fatah	Who opens	489
90	ص	Sa	Sad	Samad	Eternal	134
100	ن	Q	Qaf	Qadir	Powerful	305
200	ر	R	Ra	Rab	Lord	202
300	ش	Sh	Shin	Shafi	Who accepts	460
400	ت	T	Ta	Tawab	Who restores to good	408
500	ث	Th	Tha	Thabit	Stable	903
600	خ	Kh	Kha	Khaliq	Creator	731
700	ذ	Dh	Dhal	Dhakir	Who remembers	921
800	ض	D	Dad	Dar	Chastiser	1001
900	ظ	Dha	Dha	Dhahir	Apparent	1106
1000	غ	Gh	Gha	Ghafur	Indulgent	1285

Da'wa letter values

1	2	3	4	5	6	7	8	9	10
ا	ب	ج	د	ه	و	ز	ح	ط	ي
ك	ل	م	ن	س	ع	ف	ص	ق	ر
ش	ت	ث	خ	ذ	ض	ظ	غ		

Arabic number system

Armenian Alphabet

Before their conversion to Christianity in 301 CE, the Armenian language was mainly written using cuneiform script which was considered unsuitable for religious works by the new Christian church.

The Old Armenian alphabet was created in 405 CE by the Christian priest, Mesrop Mashtots who was given the task of searching down ancient Armenian scripts and was sent to study the principles of writing at the Egyptian city of Alexandria, where he modelled his new script on the Greek alphabet. Others include Semitic and even Ethiopian influences.

Mashtots alphabet consisted of 36 letters, 31 consonants and 7 vowels. Two extra letters being added in the 12th century to represent foreign sounds, rendering the modern 38 letter alphabet.

Although its 36 characters are thought to be an original creation, Armenian legend tells of its mystical origins, a re-invention of an older Armenian script. It is said that Mashtots was having difficulty reworking the ancient script to suit the Armenian language, until all was revealed to him by God in a dream.

This myths leads many to believe that the Armenian alphabet hides many 'cabalistic' features. As it is not just a writing system, it iss also a numerical system, used for mathematical calculations and recording calendar dates.

Each letter had two numerical values based on their alphabetical order. Its ordinal number, denoted by its place in the alphabetic sequence of letters, A = 1, B = 2. C = 3, etc.; and its cardinal number' in which the alphabet was arranged into four columns of nine rows. The first column represents the numbers 1–9, the second represents 10–90. The third row, 100–900, the fourth row, 1000–9000.

The Armenian alphabet also exhibits an Alpha-Omega like sequence which begins with A – Astvats or God and ends with Kristos or Christ. This final letter is thought to be a stylised form of the Chi-Rho symbol of early Christianity.

There are also several geometric secrets hidden in the alphabet. The first is the arrangement of the letters into an equilateral triangle. Beginning with A at the top point of the triangle and moving clockwise in rows, it places K in the bottom right corner and S in the bottom left corner of the triangle. For Christian Armenian A, K, S is a cipher to represent the Holy Trinity of the Christian Faith. A – Astvats / Father, K – Kristos/Christ and S – Sin Hogin/Holy Spirit.

If the letters are arranged inside the diamond of an octagon, reading clockwise in rows, the letters at the four corners spell out the word 'Azyk', the old native name for Armenia and its people.

A further mystery lies within the numerical order of the alphabet which appears to correspond with the atomic numbers of the chemical elements on the periodic table for the seven metals.

Using the ordinal number values for the letters, when the names of the seven metals are spelt in Armenian and converted to their ordinal number values and totalled for each word, they equal the atomic number for their equivalent chemical element in the periodic table. The periodic table wasn't invented until the 19th century.

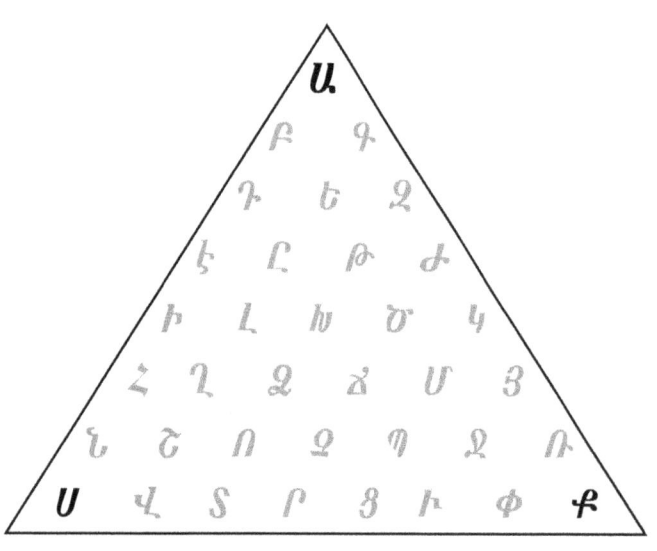

KRS - Kristos / Christ

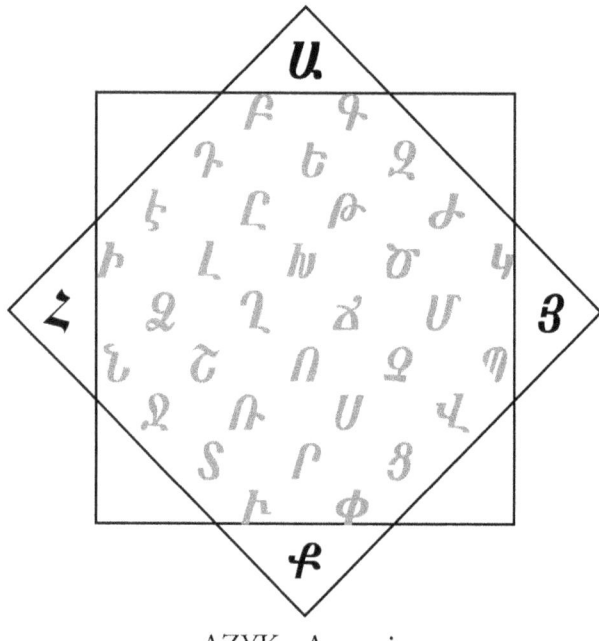

AZYK - Armenia

Cardinal Number	Ordinal Number	Capital Letter	Lowercase Letter	English Letter	Cardinal Number	Ordinal Number	Capital Letter	Lowercase Letter	English Letter
1	1	Ա	ա	A	100	19	Ծ	ծ	Tz
2	2	Բ	բ	B	200	20	Մ	մ	M
3	3	Գ	գ	G	300	21	Յ	յ	Y
4	4	Դ	դ	D	400	22	Ն	ն	N
5	5	Ե	ե	JE	500	23	Շ	շ	CH
6	6	Զ	զ	Z	600	24	Ո	ո	VO/O
7	7	Է	է	E	700	25	Չ	չ	Ts
8	8	Ը	ը	E	800	26	Պ	պ	P
9	9	Թ	թ	Th	900	27	Ջ	ջ	Dz
10	10	Ժ	ժ	Z	1000	28	Ռ	ռ	R
20	11	Ի	ի	I	2000	29	Ս	ս	S
30	12	Լ	լ	L	3000	30	Վ	վ	V
40	13	Խ	խ	Kh	4000	31	Տ	տ	T
50	14	Ծ	ծ	Ts	5000	32	Ր	ր	R
60	15	Կ	կ	K	6000	33	Ց	ց	Tsh
70	16	Հ	հ	H	7000	34	Ւ	ւ	W
80	17	Ձ	ձ	Ds	8000	35	Փ	փ	P
90	18	Ղ	ղ	R	9000	36	Ք	ք	K
							Օ	օ	OO
							Ֆ	ֆ	F

AKS

Armenian	Translation	Metal	Element	Calculation	
ՈՍԿԻ	Voski	Gold	Au - 79	Ո 21+ Ս 29+ Կ 15+ Ի 11	= 79
ԱՐԾ	Ar'ts	Silver	Ag - 47	Ա 1+ Ր 32+ Ծ 14	= 47
ԱՐՁԻԾ	Artsirs	Lead	Pb - 82	Ա 1+ Ր 32+ Ձ 19+ Ի 11+ Ձ 19	= 82
ԿԼԱԵԿ	Klaek	Tin	Sn - 50	Կ 15+ Լ 12+ Ա 1+ Է 7+ Կ 15	=50
ՋԱՆԴԻԿ	Dzandik	Mercury	Hg - 80	Ջ 27+ Ա 1+ Ն 22+ Դ 4+ Ի 11+ Կ 9	= 80
ԱԼԳԱԹ	Algath	Iron	Fe -26	Ա 1+ Լ 12+ Գ 3+ Ա 1+ Թ 9	= 26
ՄԵԴ	Med	Copper	Cu = 29	Մ 20+ Ե 5+ Դ 4	= 29

Metals and Atomic Numbers

Runic Futhark

The Runic Futhark is the alphabet of the pre-Christian, Germanic peoples of northern Europe. In the Norse pagan tradition, runes were employed as a mystic symbol system before they were adapted to a writing system, which began around 500 BCE. The Futhark reached a peak of use between the 4th and 7th centuries CE, before being slowly replaced by the Latin alphabet. Their use as a script ended in 17th century Iceland.

Runes were rediscovered and revived during the 18th and 19th centuries by the Romantic movement, and again in the 20th century by the neopagan movement. The futhark is written in runic script ('runic' meaning 'carved' or 'scratched'), as runes are traditionally carved or scratched into wood and rock.

The word 'rune' means 'a mystery' in Old Norse and their origins lie in the archaic pictographic symbolism linked to divination practices in sun, tree and fertility cults, particularly those found at Hallristningar in Sweden, dating from before the end of the second Bronze Age, 1300 BCE. These symbols are known as Ur-Runes (Urrunen), which refers to runes before they became systemized.

Germanic ancestral lore sings of an ancient tribe known as the Volsungr, who wondered out of the far north with the last great Ice Age. They were the guardians of the primordial forests and ancient trackways. It was also the task of the Volsungr to seed the knowledge of the Ur-Runes among the newer tribes who would maintain their mysteries. Once this task was completed, they withdrew into the deepest, holiest northern forests and passed beyond human knowledge.

Like the word 'alphabet', the word 'Futhark' is derived from the letter values of its first six letters.

From about 100 BCE to 1600 CE, three main Futharks were in use. The oldest and original is the Germanic, Common or Elder Futhark, followed by the Anglo-Saxon Futhorc and the Norse or Scandinavian Younger Futhark. They were written either left to right, right to left, top to bottom, bottom to top or in a circle.

The letter names of the Futhark follows the acrophonic principle, in which the initial sound of the name is the sound value of the rune: F-Freya, H-Hagel. etc. The runic names are meaningful and linked to certain trees for calendar-making.

The runic calendar is a lunar-solar calendar with the 24 runes employed to mark the 24 hours of the day and night, phases of the Moon and represent the two halves of a solar month. It is used to mark the solstices, equinoxes, eclipses, and Christian holidays and feasts.

The oldest runic calendar known is a medieval Swedish example. The concept of a runic calendar took place in an era when writing was still considered a magic art. Those who held its knowledge of the runes had access to the primal inherent workings of the universe and natural world.

The alphabetization of runes began during the 5th century BCE, when the Alpengermanen (Alpine-Germans) are thought to have come into contact with the Latin alphabet. At this point, there occurred a fusion between the Germanic Ur-Runes and letters from the North Italian alphabets, specifically Alpine Etruscan.

By 100 BCE, this resulted in the creation of the 24 rune staves known as the Germanic, Common or Elder Futhark. The reason for this fusion may have been to preserve the runes for times when magical symbols would be increasingly used for written communication and records. But it should be said that even after the systemization, rune staves continued to be used primarily for magical purposes rather than for writing, and never developed a cursive form.

During the 1st century BCE, the Elder Futhark journeyed northward and eastward down the Rhine, along the North Sea coastal route by way of the Frisian Islands and Heligoland Bay, and from there to Schleswig-Holstein to reach Denmark, Jutland and Scandinavia by the 3rd century CE.

In the 6th century, the Elder Futhark developed a Danish/Friesian variant of 28 staves called the Anglo-Saxon Futhorc. It continued to develop, reaching a total of 33 runic staves in the early 9th century.

Use of the pagan Elder and Anglo-Saxon Futharks came to an end early in the 9th century; replaced by the Christian, Latin alphabet. After a period of transition, an entirely Norse or Scandinavian rune-row of 16 staves came into being, known as the Younger Futhark.

In Scandinavia, runes remained in use until the 16th century in Gotland, the 17th century in Iceland and runic calendars were still in use in remote regions of Sweden and Iceland into the 19th century. In the 1970s, Icelandic pagans of Asatru or Native Faith adapted runic script to write the Latin alphabet.

Ur-Runen - 1300 BCE

Ur-Runen with a known phonetic value

U/V	W	H	N	J	e(ei)	Z	T	M	Ng	O	D

Alpine Etruscan - 650 BCE

| F | U/V | A | R | K | H | N | I | P | Z | S | T | E | M | L | Ng |

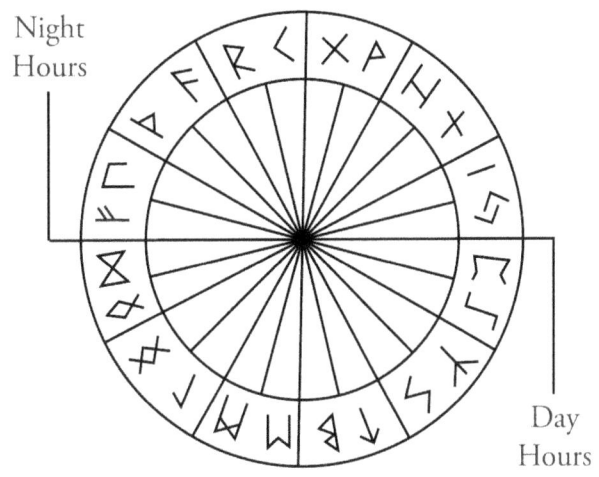

Rune Wheel - Circular and Cyclical order
(alphabet, almanac, calender, sun dial, birth chart, etc.)

Germanic, Common or Elder Futhark - 100 BCE

F U Th A R K G W H N I J E(ei) P Z S T B E M L Ng O D

Anglo/Saxon Futhorc - 500 CE

F U Th O R C G W H N I J Y(ei) P Z S T B E M L Ng O D A AE Y(r) IO EA st cc c

Norse or Younger Futhark - 850 CE

F U Th A R K H N I O S T B M L Y

Icelandic runes - 1970s

A B C D E F G H I J K L M N P Q R S T X Y Th AE OO

Rune Staves

Rune staves began as symbols that made up words or names. The stave is the straight line around which the defining elements of the rune are placed. The placement of runic elements around a stave is called binding. However, the original rune meaning may no longer be recognizable as the creator often wanted to conceal their work.

Binding creates a magical rune arrangement that increases their power and creates magic formulas. The binding of letters that formed spells into mystical symbols was a popular practice throughout the Greek and Roman empires and was just as important to the Norse.

Rune staves were used mainly on amulets to cast spells, cure illness, and attract love and fortune or as a form of protection in battle and for safety when travelling or fishing. The rune sequence ALU is the most common runic charm of old. Those used to foretell the future are called prophetic runes.

The Roman historian Tacitus recorded in 98 CE, that Drottirs or Druids were taking auspices and casting lots using rune staves incised into discs of nut wood or pebbles and coloured red. These were thrown at random onto a white cloth whilst the gods were invoked. The priest took three sticks or stones, one at a time from the cloth, interpreting the sigils accordingly.

'Blotspann' is the name given to the method of divination which involves casting three wooden chips inscribed with runes into a bowl containing the blood of sacrificed animals to obtain warnings and see into the future.

There are different types of rune stave, the most common bind forms are linear and stacked. Other common forms are radial or cartwheel formations. Highly elaborate cartwheel designs often resemble snowflake shapes whose elements include modifiers, meaningful marks drawn over the body of staves.

The runes of the futhark can be combined to forge special symbols called linear and stacked bind runes and include each rune needed to encompass the intention of the spell for making amulets and charms. They are concept runes; instead of writing the words out in full, the rune master uses bind runes to express all that they wanted to say in one symbol.

Sventhorn are the most authentic of Viking symbols, mentioned many times in Nordic saga's including the saga of the Volsungs, the saga of King Hrolf Kraki and the saga of Gongu-Hrolf. Although the appearance, definition and magical qualities of the Sventhorn is somewhat different in every myth, they do have one thing in common. In all the stories, Sventhorn were used by Norse gods and their people to put their adversaries into a deep, long sleep.

Galdrastafir (magic staves) are the most complex form of rune staves. It is the name given to the hundreds of Icelandic magical rune staves, a mixture of Viking and Christian magic, that appeared between 1400 and 1800, most from the 1600s. They are found in 17th century 'black' grimoires like the Huld manuscript. Some intermix Christian and Viking elements, others are solely Christian related. It is likely that Galdrastafir appeared in Iceland after other symbols were seen in medieval grimoires from mainland Europe. They are most likely influenced by the Keys of Solomon, as they contain sigils to banish demons and such.

Since the 1800s, Galdrastafir have been drawn and redrawn, many are missing or with added elements that change how the original looked. They were revived in the 19th century by the Geatish Society and re-revived as symbols associated with the Scandinavian Heathenism called Asatru in the 1970s and 80s. Although they do not originate from the Viking Age, they are steeped in Norse mythology and Scandinavian folklore, with connections to the gods and goddesses and runic characters going back centuries.

Galdrastafir can be divided into two separate forms; asymmetrical which are the older forms, created using the common method of sigil work for names and magic; and the later symmetrical forms which have a greater esotericism and range, from the simplest to the very complex and elaborate forms, some of which resemble snowflake patterns.

The designs of Galdrastafir can be seen as a graphic representation of a magic spell or incantation, whose purpose can range from acquiring good fortune and protection in life to more sinister spells for raising the dead, causing ill health and even death.

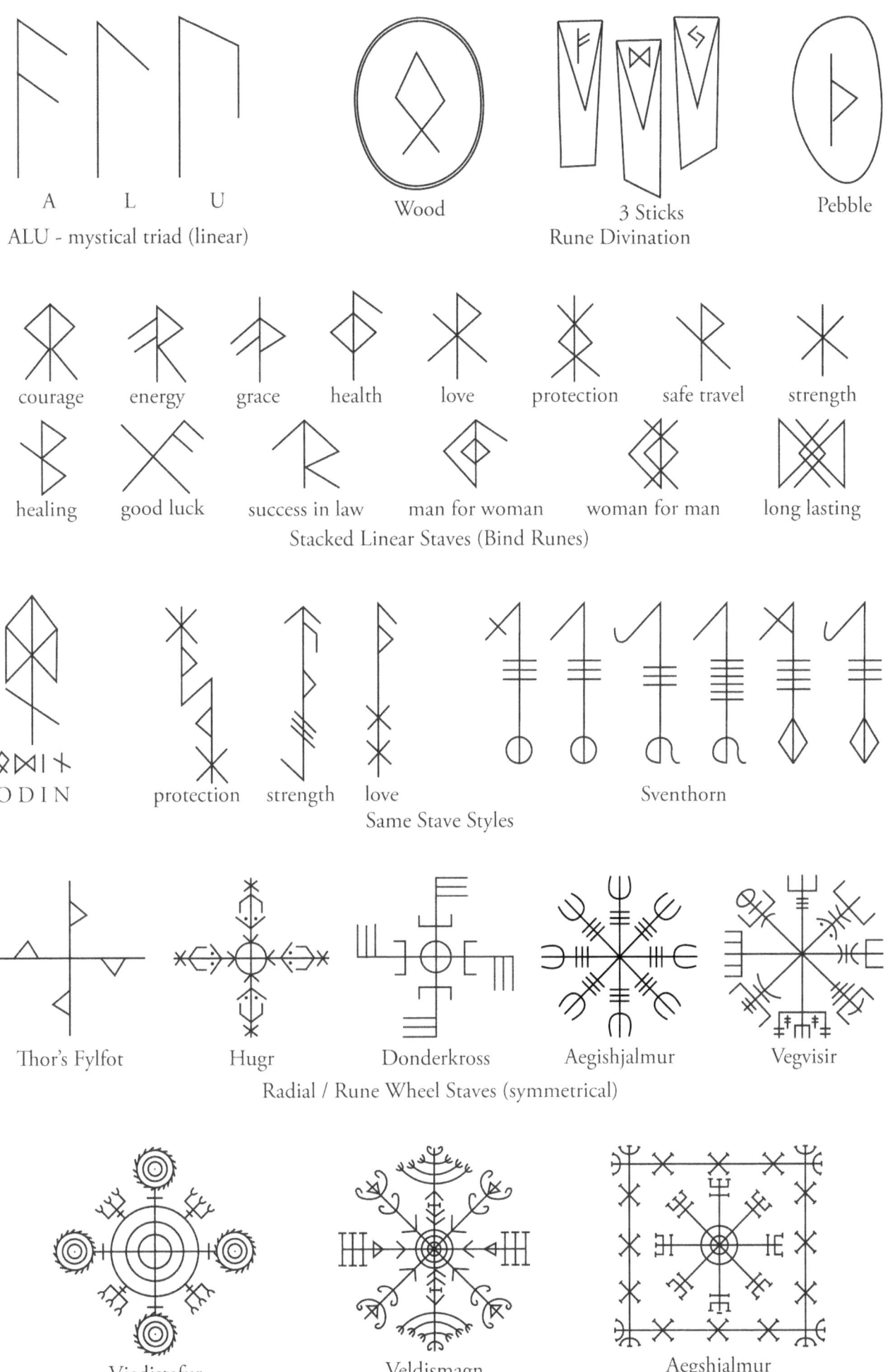

Runic Oracle

Runes are symbols created with magical intent, and therefore all letters are considered magical by nature. In this oracle system, the runes represent the forces of nature and mind from which one seeks advice.

The runes were not invented, they were and are seen as pre-existing forces handed down from eternity. They are considered intrinsically magic by their very nature. They promoted communication, not only between men but between mankind and deities, allowing for a conversation with the hidden powers that animate the world.

In the Norse mystical tradition, each runic letter has several attributes; an alphabetical value, a numerical value, a pictorial representation (Fehu is based on the depiction of a cattle skull), a divinatory one, an aural one (the chanting or singing of the rune's name for meditation and prayer) and a definitive one, as well as correspondences to trees and plants. Reversed or inverted runes carry negative connotations.

In runic mysticism, everything that exists is seen as being connected in a vast web called the Web of the Wyrd, Skuld's Net or the Matrix of Fate. Originally, the web was represented as a beautiful symmetrical spider's web, centered on the North Star. Later, it conspired that the Nornir, Norns or Three Fates had woven the web, a construct of nine staves symmetrically arranged on an angular grid, a symbol that represents the interconnectedness and interdependency between the past, present and future.

The Web of the Wyrd is sometimes envisioned with Yggdrasil, the Cosmic Tree, at the center of the universe, connecting all the Nine Realms. Norse mythology tells that whilst hanging upside down on Yggdrasil, Odin took the nine staves of the Cosmic Law of Creation or the Web of the Wyrd and cast them to the ground, where they formed the patterns that revealed the 24 runic staves of the Elder Futhark to him.

For divination purposes, the 24 runes of the Futhark were divided into 3 lots of 8 called families or Aetirs, each was assigned to a god. Freya's eight, Hegel's eight and Tiw's eight.

The runic oracle has seen many incarnations since the 18th century Viking revival of Scandanavian romantic nationalism (Gothicumis). German occultism in the 19th century and European neopaganism in the 20th century.

In the modern runic oracle, the Futhark converts into the equivalent of the cabala, tarot or the I-Ching. Beginning in the 17th century when Johannes Bureus, a Hermeticist and Rosicrucian developed a runic system called Adulrunen or Noble runes, employing cabalistic numerology that corresponds to the Younger Futhark.

Throughout the 19th and early 20th centuries, the runic oracle was developed by contemporary adherents of German mysticism. Rune master, Werner Kosab's 56-stave 'Das Runen Orikal' combines modern runes with older forms and symbols derived from the Hermetic tradition.

In 1902, Austrian mystic, Guido von List, developed a system of Aryan cabala. According to List, the 18 characters of his runic alphabet were the most ancient script of the Ayran race, being older than the 24 runes of the Elder Futhark. He named them Armanen, the archaic name for Germany. List also identified each of his runes with one of the 18 spells of the old Norse poem 'Havamal' in the Poetic Edda, giving them magical meaning.

Germany's defeat in WWI led some German occultists to see the runes as a significant part of German national identity, which led to the appropriation of runes by the Nazi party.

Armenan runes reached a height of influence when Hitler ordered Nazi occultist, Karl Maria Wiligut, to develop their everyday use for writing the German language, after being told of the Semitic heritage of the Latin alphabet. They are still used today in esoteric and German neopaganism.

Following WWII runes fell into disrepute, reappearing in the late 1960s with a revival in rune magic by such folk as JRR Tolkien, Counter Culture hippies and the emerging neopagans of the post-war world.

From the 1980s onwards, several more modern systems of runic divination were published. The first of these books was written in 1980 by Ralph Blum. His system employs the runes of the Elder Futhark plus a blank, making 25, arranged in five rows of five. The runes are either selected one by one from a closed bag or thrown down at random for a reading.

As well as introducing the blank rune, Blum pioneered the direct correlation between the runes and the tarot cards, with the inclusion of rune cards and spreads.

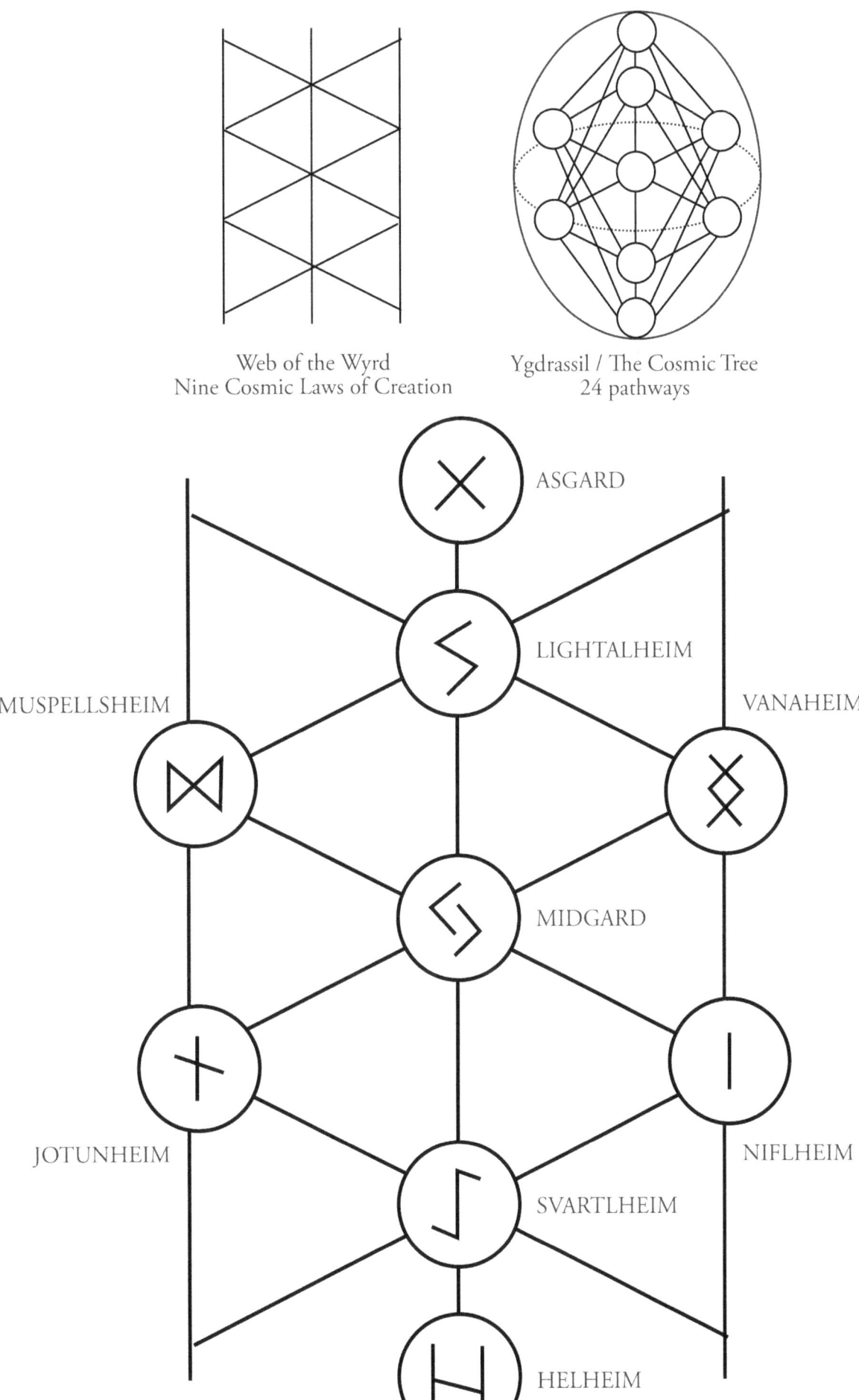

Web of the Wyrd, Ygdrassil and the nine realms

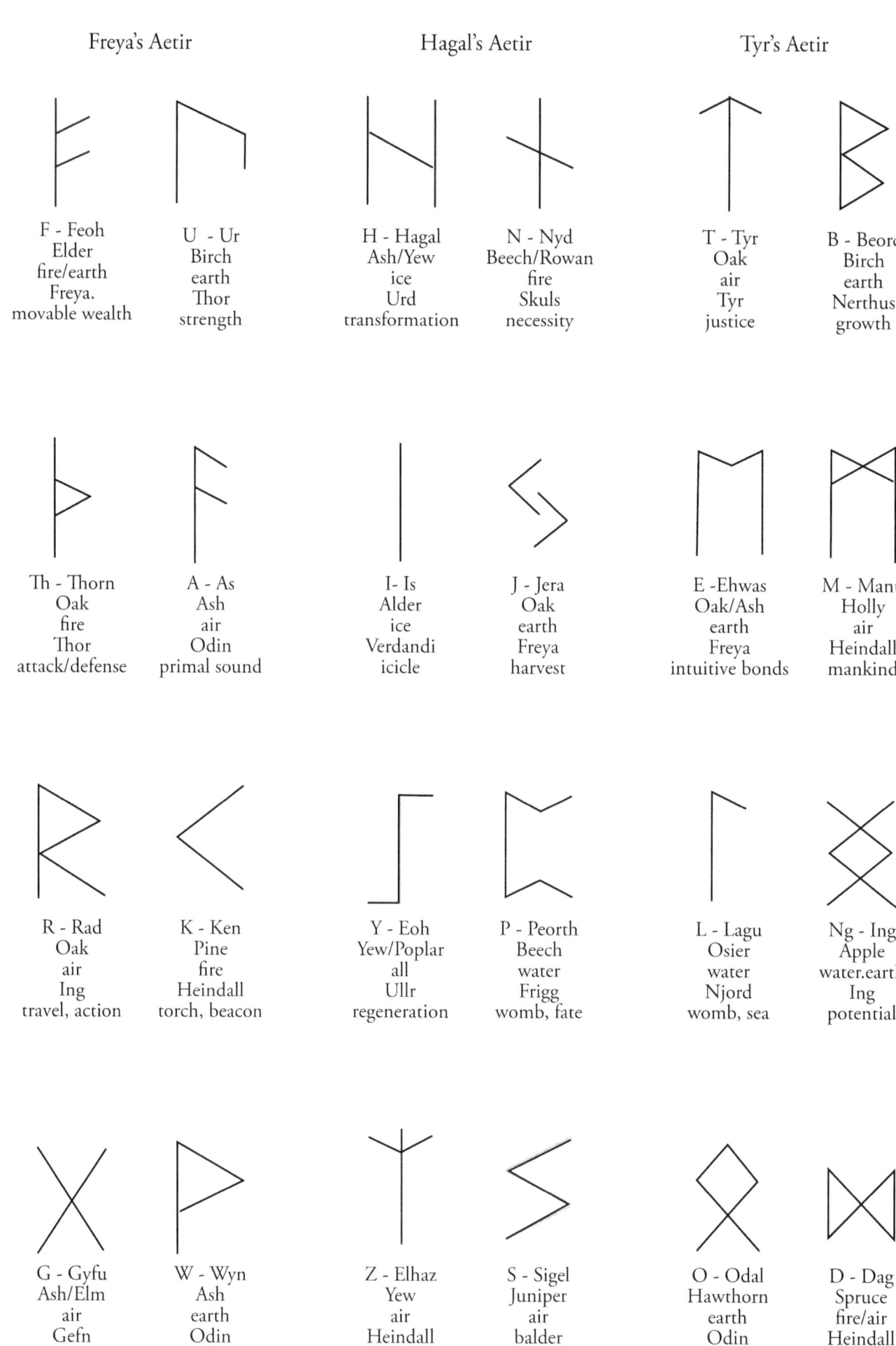

Elder Futhark Aetir's or families and correspondences

Sound	Rune	Name	Tree	Element	Deity	Meaning
A		Ac	Oak	fire	Thor	potential
AE		Os	Ash	air	Odin	speech
Y(r)		Ur	Yew	all	Odin/Frigg	bow
IO		Iur	Ivy	water	Njord	world serpent
EA		Ear	Yew	earth	Hela	death

4th Aetir

Sound	Rune	Name	Tree	Element	Deity	Meaning
c		Cweorth	bay/beech	fire	Loge	funeral pyre
cc		Calc	maple	earth	Norns	grail
st		Stan	witch hazel	earth	Nerthus	sacred stone
g		Gar	ash/spindle	all	Odin	spear of Odin
		Wolfsangel	yew	earth	Vidar	wolf hook
		Ziu	oak	air/fire	Tyr	thunderbolt
		Erda	elder/birch	earth	Erda	Mother Earth
		Ul	blackthorn	air	Waldh	turning point
		Sol	juniper	fire	Sol	the Sun

5th Aetir

Anglo-Saxon additions

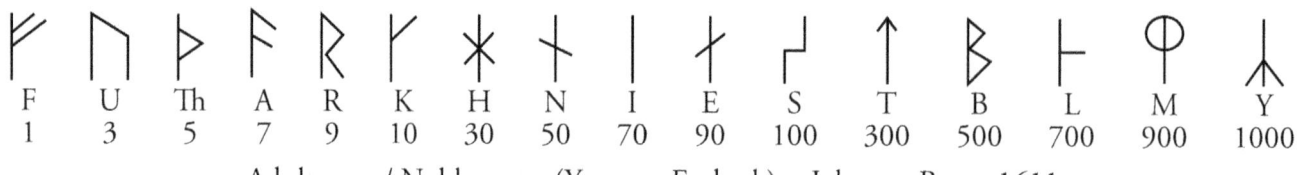

Adulrunen / Noble runes (Younger Futhark) - Johames Burus 1611

F - Fa - generate your luck and you will have it

U - Ur - know yourself, then you will know all

Th - Thurs - preserve your ego

A / O - Os - your spirit force makes you free

R - Rit - I am right, this rod right is indestructable, therefore, I am indestructable

K - Ka - your blood, your highest possession

H - Hag - harbour the All in yourself and you will control the All

N - Nor - use your fate, do not strive against it

I - Is - win power over youself and you will have power over everything in the spiritual and physical world

A - Ar - respect the primal fire

S - Sig - the creative spirit must conquer

T - Tyr - fear not death, it cannot kill you

B - Bar - the life strands in the hands of God, trust it in you

L - Laf - first learn to steer, then do the sea journey

M - Man - be a man

Y - Yr - think about the end

E - Em - marriage is the raw-root of the Aryan

G - Gibor - Man, be one with God

Armenan runes (Aryan cabala) Von List, 1902

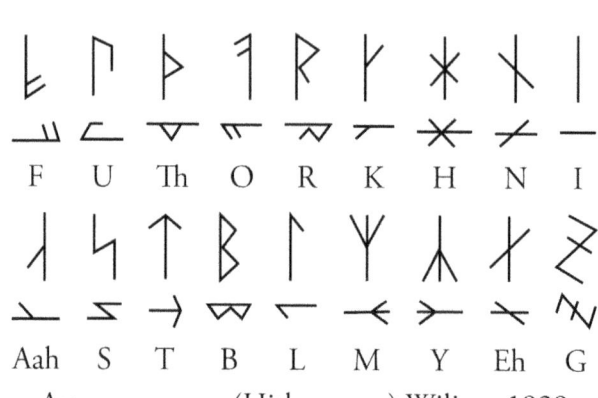

Armanen runes (Hitler runes) Wiligut 1929
horizontal and vertical variants

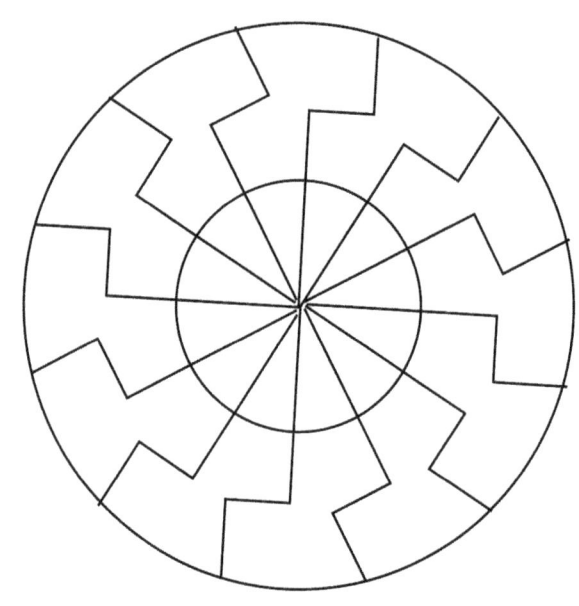

Sig Rune Wheel (Black Sun)

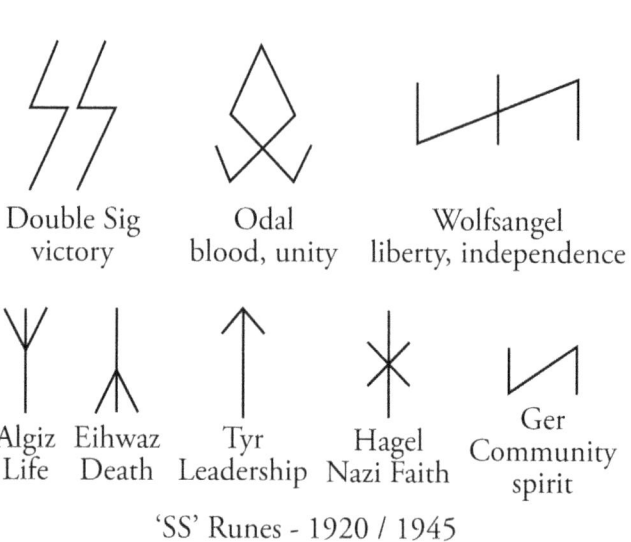

Double Sig — victory
Odal — blood, unity
Wolfsangel — liberty, independence

Algiz — Life
Eihwaz — Death
Tyr — Leadership
Hagel — Nazi Faith
Ger — Community spirit

'SS' Runes - 1920 / 1945

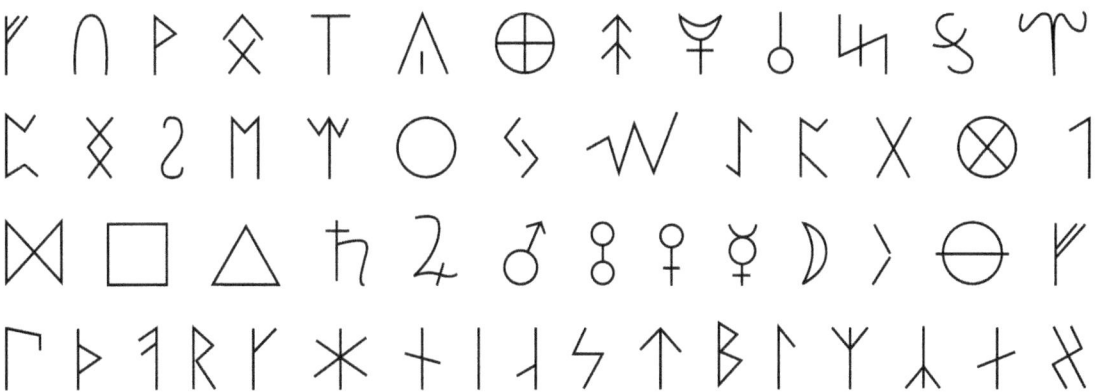

"Das Runen Orikal" - Werner Kosab

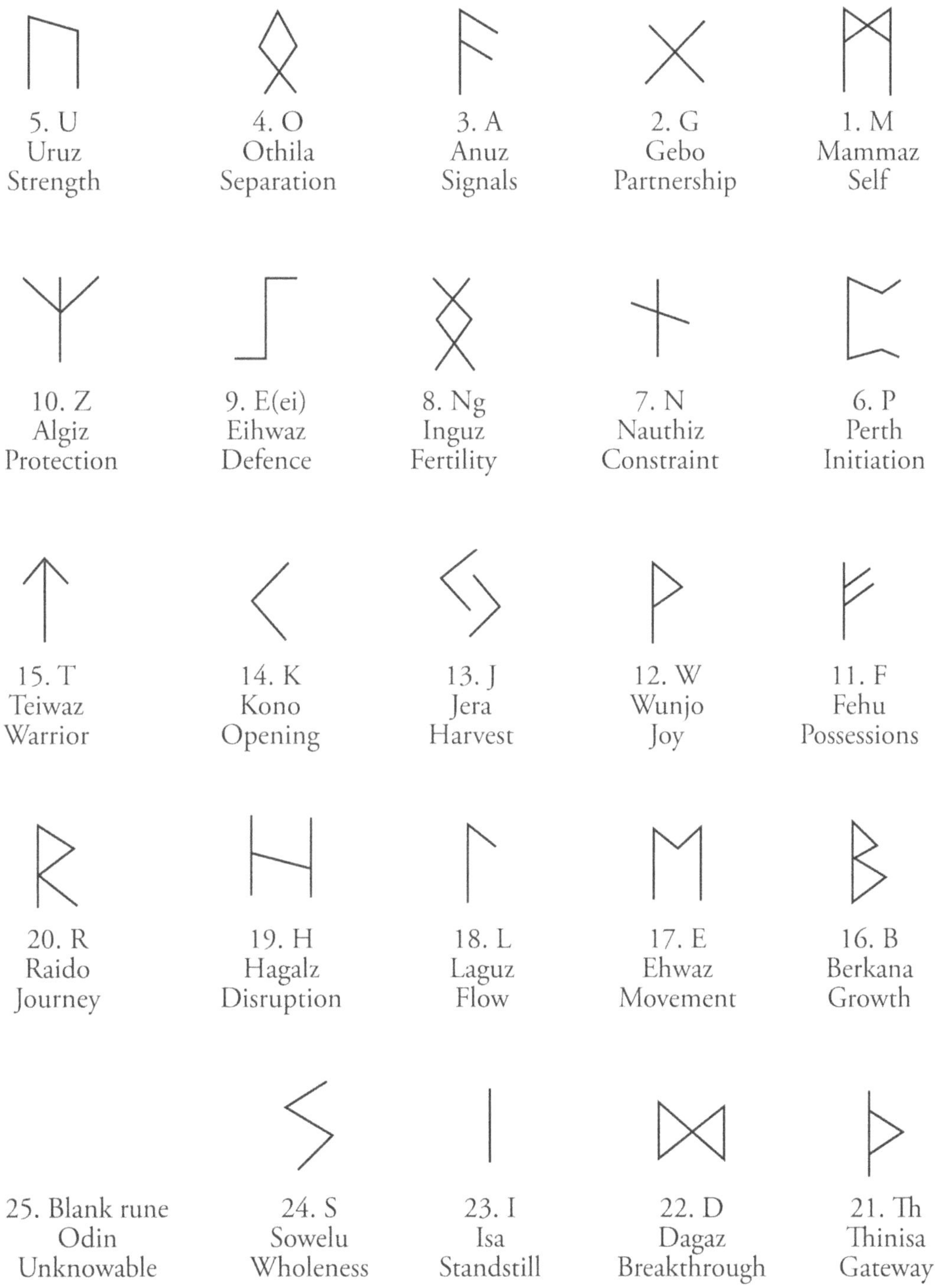

5. U Uruz Strength	4. O Othila Separation	3. A Anuz Signals	2. G Gebo Partnership	1. M Mammaz Self
10. Z Algiz Protection	9. E(ei) Eihwaz Defence	8. Ng Inguz Fertility	7. N Nauthiz Constraint	6. P Perth Initiation
15. T Teiwaz Warrior	14. K Kono Opening	13. J Jera Harvest	12. W Wunjo Joy	11. F Fehu Possessions
20. R Raido Journey	19. H Hagalz Disruption	18. L Laguz Flow	17. E Ehwaz Movement	16. B Berkana Growth
25. Blank rune Odin Unknowable	24. S Sowelu Wholeness	23. I Isa Standstill	22. D Dagaz Breakthrough	21. Th Thinisa Gateway

Viking Runic Oracle of Robert Blum

Tree Ogham

Tree Ogham is the common name for the Celtic writing system that takes the initial letter of the names of trees and arranges them in sequential order for calendar-making and is used as an alphabet. The origin of this botanical system has its roots in the seasonal plants, shrubs and trees found in the Rhineland, home of the ancestral Iron Age Celtic 'La Terne' culture.

Tree calendars were common in the Bronze Age, employed from Palestine to Ireland and universally associated with the triple-moon goddess of the 3-season lunar year, before being adapted to act as the 4-season, solar calendar of the Sun God.

The word Ogham, pronounced Oh-m or Oh-wam, means 'language' or 'eloquence'. It is named after Oghma, the Celtic god of poetry and eloquence. He is said to have invented Ogham script as a way of recording poetry and to show how clever he was, although there is no evidence to suggest that Ogham was ever used to write poetry.

Most of what we known of Tree Ogham is explained by Robert Graves in his book 'The White Goddess', where he explains the mystical arrangement and numerology contained within it. He reveals that it contains the original order of the letters of the alphabet, derived from the lunar zodiac, represented by trees arranged in sequential order that are sacred to the Moon or White Goddess.

Much of what is written by Graves is disputed by scholars and divinationists alike. There is no proof that Tree Ogham acted as a calendar in the way that Graves suggests, but as all alphabets have a single origin, it stands to reason that Ogham should contain all the wisdom of the original alphabet.

As a writing system, Tree Ogham was originally an alphabet of 20 letters, increased to 25 with the addition of 5 extra letters to write Greek words in Irish. It died out around 500 CE, replaced by the Latin alphabet. It represents the sounds of Celtic language by using a series of ordered lines or branches, that emanate from either side or across a central line or stave.

This script style is thought to be graphically derived from Tree Ogham, one of many Ogham systems employed by Celtic Druids. Most Ogham systems were number ciphers (which may account for the scripts' resemblance to tally marks), all of which could be communicated using Ogham sign language, in which different finger signs are stroked along the ridge of the nose or shin to communicate.

The tally arrays of Ogham script form individual letters called fews. In the Tree Ogham alphabet, there are 20 fews representing the months, equinoxes and solstices of the lunar and solar calendars. They are set out in 4 sets of 5 called 'Groves', representing the seasons.

Theoretically, Ogham consonants could be used to mark a henge or dolmen to form a calendar. The left post for spring, the right for autumn and the lintel for summer. The five vowels, with the addition of two extra vowels AA and II, formed the threshold of the dolmen, representing New Year's Day. With the two extra vowels, the total number of strokes of the Ogham alphabet equals 72, the number of lunar wisdom.

Tree Ogham differs from cabala, in that cabala has one tree, whereas Ogham has a 'grove' filled with many trees and woodland plants. The Celts believed that humans were descended from trees and because of this, trees played an important role in their religious beliefs.

Ogham was used for divination, fortune-telling and writing curses and charms. As a divination system, Ogham fews are carved into slivers of wood or staves and thrown on to a cloth where the spread is interpreted. Historically, they were incised on four yew wands. The modern diviner cuts them into staves of wood, which are then stored in a bag or pouch. The questioner must take a minimum of 3 staves from the bag and cast them on the floor. The closest represents the past, the ones in the middle show the present and those furthest away reveal the future.

Charms were written on elm wands which were used to strike the client to activate the charm. Curses were often written on rods of aspen, as everything hateful was written on it.

There are few examples in literature of Ogham being used for magical purposes. The best-known of these is in the tale of Tochmark Etaine, when the Druid Dallan locates the missing Etaine through inscribing Ogham fews on four rods of yew.

Number	Irish name	Letter	Ogham	English name	Date
5	Beth	B		Birch	Dec 25
14	Luis	L		Rowan	Jan 21
13	Nion	N		Ash	Feb 18
8	Fearn	F(V)		Alder	Mar 18
16	Saile	S		Willow	Apr 15
7	Uath	H		Whitethorn	May 12
12	Duir	D		Oak	Jun 10
11	Tinne	T		Holly	Jul 8
9	Coll	C		Hazel	Aug 5
	Quert	Q		Apple	Aug 5
6	Muin	M		Vine	Sept 2
10	Gort	G		Ivy	Sep 30
7	Ngetal/Peth	Ng/Gn/P		Reed/Dwarf Elder	Oct 28
	Straif	Z/FF(F)		Blackthorn	Apr 15
15	Ruis	R		Elder	Nov 25
	Palm	AA/Omega		Palm	New Years Day
1	Alim	A		Silver Fir	New Year
4	Onn	O		Gorse/Furze	Spring equinox
	Ura	U		Heather	Summer solstice
2	Eadha	E		White Poplar	Autumn equinox
3	Idhu	I		Yew	Winter solstice
		II, J, Y		Mistletoe	Dec 23

BLN variant of the Tree Ogham alphabet

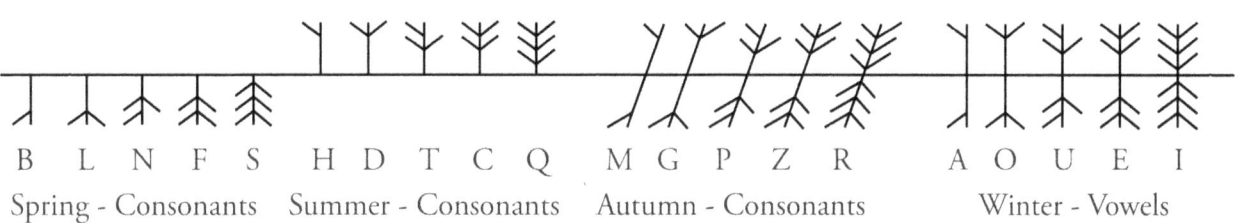

Horizontal Branching Ogham - Fews and Groves

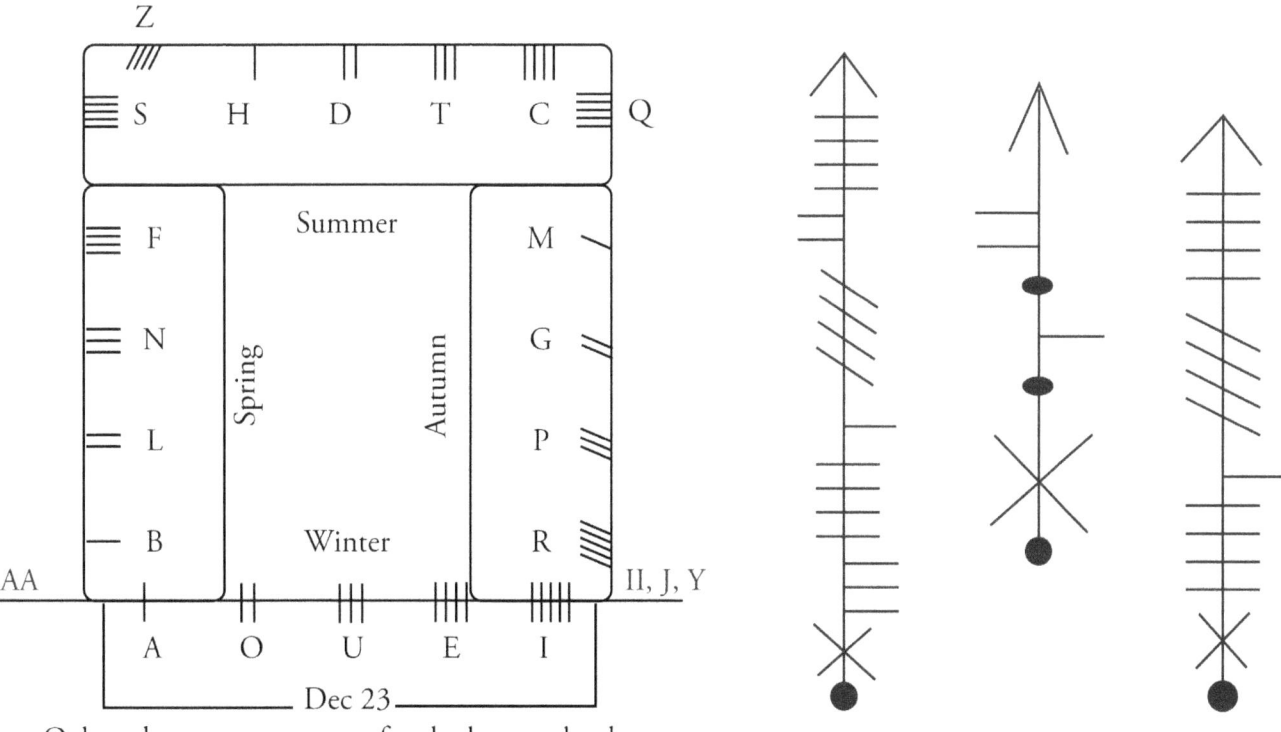

Ogham henge arrangement for the lunar calender

Ogham Staves

Enochian Alphabet

Between 1581 and 1587, the Enochian language, alphabet and script were all allegedly transmitted by angels to the Renaissance occultists, Sir Edward Kelly, a psychic medium, and Dr. John Dee, court astrologer to Elizabeth I. They employed them in their system of ritual magic known as Enochian.

The Enochian system is based on the invocation and evocation of the various tutelary spirits of the nations and is considered powerful in comparison to most other magical systems. Aleister Crowley deemed the Enochian system to be too powerful and stopped using it.

Dee and Kelly were told by the angels that the magic would give superhuman powers to its practitioners, change the political structure of Europe and herald the coming of the apocalypse. Dee believed that what he was doing would be of benefit to posterity and documented the instructions into a series of manuscripts and workbooks.

The term Enochian comes from Dee's assertion that the Biblical Patriarch, Enoch, had been the last human to know the language before he and Kelly. Dee preferred the title Angelical or Celestial speech, the language of the Angels, the first language of the God-Christ, the Holy language, used in the Garden of Eden by Adam to speak with God and to name all things in existence.

Angelical was hidden from humans with the exception of the Biblical Patriarch, Enoch, who wrote the Book of Loageath, 'Speech from God', for humanity but it was lost in the deluge of Noah.

Enochian linguistic structure is based on an alphabetical cipher for an angelic language that is recorded using a unique script formed of 21 letters, neither capitals or lowercase, written from right to left as in Hebrew. Its authenticity is disputed by linguists who liken it to an Anglicized version of Hebrew.

It was revealed to Kelly during 'scrying' sessions, when various texts and tables were revealed to them by angels. Scrying is a technique used to tell the future and involves gazing into a reflective surface such as a black obsidian mirror or a crystal ball to receive messages. They would watch the mirror or ball and record everything they saw and heard.

Kelly, as the receiver of the language, wrote his texts in Enochian, the resulting book is called Liber Loageath, 'Book of the Speech from God'. The book consisted of 49 great letter tables of 49 x 49 letters. Each having a front and a backside making 98 49 x 49 tables in all.

A year later, Kelly received a second set of texts comprised of 48 poetic verses Dee called 'Claves Angelicea' or Angelic Keys. They are the keys to open the 49 gates of wisdom represented by the 49 magic squares in the Liber Loageath.

There are three slightly different versions of their Enochian script. Dee's version was published first in the Five Books of the Mysteries. Kelly's version, the original and more accepted, was published in the Liber Loagaeth. Aleister Crowley created a third version for the Hermetic Order of the Golden Dawn.

The letters of the Enochian alphabet also have correspondences with Dr. Rudd's geomantic characters, the only source that combines sixteen Enochian letters with geomantic characters, although five of these letters do not have any correspondences to a geomantic character.

It is said that the angels warned Dee and Kelly never to perform Enochian magic until the time was right. It is believed both died without ever using it. Their work was just information, it was not a system of any usable value. As such, it remained dormant, undefined and useable, although it did have some influence on the Rosicrucian's.

For some 200 years. Dee and Kelly's works lay dormant in the British Library until rediscovered and given form by the Hermetic Order of the Golden Dawn in the 1880's. Golden Dawn member, S L Macgregor Mathers developed Dee and Kelly's Enochian material into the comprehensive system of Ceremonial magic used today.

The list of correspondences and analogies are a vital part of practical Angelic magic. Only a little is known about the correspondences of Dee's Enochian symbolic system. There are different types of Gematria used in the Enochian system from the Greek/Hebrew numerology to those of the Aurum Solis and Aleister Crowley.

Alphabet	Script	Name	Number	Angel	Inteligence	Tarot	Zodiac
A		Un	6	Asmodel	Kedemel	Heirophant	Taurus
B		Pa	5	Malchidael	Barzabel	Star	Aries
D		Gal	300		Tapthatarath	Judgement	Fire
E		Graph	4 / 31	Hamaliel	Barazbel	Empress	Spirit
F		Or	10			Hermit	Virgo
G, J		Ged	3	Verchiel	Scrath	Magician	Cauda Draconis
H		Na	8			Chariot	Cancer
I, Y		Gon	1	Advachiel	Hismael	Fool	Air
C K		Veh	60			Temperence	Sagitarius
L		Ur	8	Muriel	Hasmodai	Chariot	Cancer
M		Tal	90	Cambriel	Jismael	Emperor	Aquarius
N		Drux	50	Baeachiel		Death	Scorpio
O		Med	30	Euriel	Barzabel	Jistice	Libra
P		Mals	9	Miroel	Kademel	Lovers	Leo
Q		Ger	40		Hasmodai	Hanged man	Water
R		Don	100	Annixiel	Hismael	Moon	Pisces
S		Fam	7	Ambtiel	Thathatarath	Lovers	Gemini
T		Gisg	9 / 3		Kedemal	Lovers	Leo
U V W		Van	70	Hanael	Zazel	Devil	Capricorn
X		Pal	400			Universe	Earth
Z		Ceph	9 / 3	Advachiel	Svtay	High Priestess	Caput Dranconis

Enochian alphabet, script and correspondences - Hermetic Order of the Golden Dawn

Geomantic Characters

The word 'Geomantic' is an amalgamation of the Latin word's 'geo' meaning 'earth' and 'mantia' meaning 'divination'.

Geomancy is a system of divination that uses the random generation of points in a dot system to divine the hidden meanings from the earth. It is often associated with the oriental art of Feng Shui and is also referred to as the Western I-Ching. It is a very archaic divination practice, heavily influenced by astrology, which makes it possible for Geomantic figures to be assigned to a letter of the alphabet, particularly the letters of the Enochian alphabet.

A contemporary of Dr. John Dee and Sir Edward Kelly, Dr. Rudd's system is the only source of all that combines the sixteen Geomantic characters with the Enochian symbols and angels, although five of these symbols do not have any correspondences to a Geomantic character.

The system came to Europe from the Middle East, where it was called Khatt al-rami, 'cutting the sand'. It uses the random generation of marks or dots to create a four-line figure, one line for each of the elements, the divinatory meaning of the figure depending upon the number and arrangement of the dots.

The 16 Geomantic figures are an abstract binary system of four lines of dots, with either one or two dots in each line. A line containing a single dot is considered negative, a line with two dots signifies positive. The four lines are called the head, neck, body and feet, and they are each assigned an element; head – fire, neck – air, body – water, feet – earth.

The most common technique used to produce a Geomantic figure lets a diviner create a series of holes or dots or points in the earth (or more properly a box containing sacred or blessed earth), from left to right in a line, until there are four individual lines of randomly created dots. The dots in each line are counted. If they total an even number then they are a represented by two dots. If the total is an odd or uneven number then it is represented by a single dot, thereby creating a Geometric figure.

The 16 figures represent the 16 possible elemental states of anything. The elemental structure is the framework of meaning for figure, but plenty of other symbols and ideas have been added to them by Geomancers of the millennia.

The first four figures in the series are called the mothers or matres. The next four are called the daughters or fillae. From the mothers and daughters come the four nephews. These 12 figures are each assigned to a constellation of the Zodiac. Since there are only twelve signs of the Zodiac and 16 Geomantic figures, four signs have two figures assigned to them. From the nephews come the two witnesses or testes and from these comes a single judge or judex.

They all have a Latin name and a keyword which help to cast light on the wider meaning of the symbol. Each figure has an inner or ruling element that the figure expresses most intensely.

They also have an outer element, usually different from the inner element which shows the figure's expression in the world around it. For instance, Fortuna Major has fire as its inner element, which represents the power to reshape the world in a favourable way. Its outer element is earth, which means its power comes not from rushing around, but from establishing itself solidly and letting everything else move around it.

The figures are also divided by quality, either mobile or stable. For example, if something is lost or stolen, a stable figure means the item will be recovered, while a mobile figure means it is gone for good.

A Geomantic character is a picture, image, symbol or ideogram, created by connecting the dots of an individual figure using lines. These characters are used in the creation of amulets and talismans for their power in association with their planetary ruler. Fourteen of the figures are assigned to the seven visible planets of our solar system. The two others are assigned to the lunar nodes, the two points in space where the eclipses happen.

Letter	Matrix	Character	Name and Meaning	Ruling Planet/Element	Planetary Characters
A		△△	Amissio - loss	Venus	
B		◇	Puer - boy	Mars	
D		|	-	air	
E		⊠	Conjunctio - assembly	Mercury	
F		△	Cauda Draconis - dragon's tail	Lunar node	
G, J		目	Populus - people	Moon	
H		○	-	air	
I, Y		⊗	Aquisto - gain	Jupiter	
C, K		△	-	fire	
L		⊖	Via - way	Moon	
M		日	Tristitia - sorrow	Saturn	
N		囚	Rebeus - red	Mars	
O		◇	Puella - girl	Venus	
P		▽	Fortuna Major - greater fortune	Sun	
Q		▽	-	water	
R		⌂	Laetitia - joy	Jupiter	
S		▽	Albus - white	Mercury	
T		▽	Caput Draconis - dragon's head	Lunar node	
U, V, W		◇	Carcer - prison	Saturn	
X		□	-	earth	
Z		△△	Fortuna Minor - lesser fortune	Sun	

Geomantic / Enochian correspondences

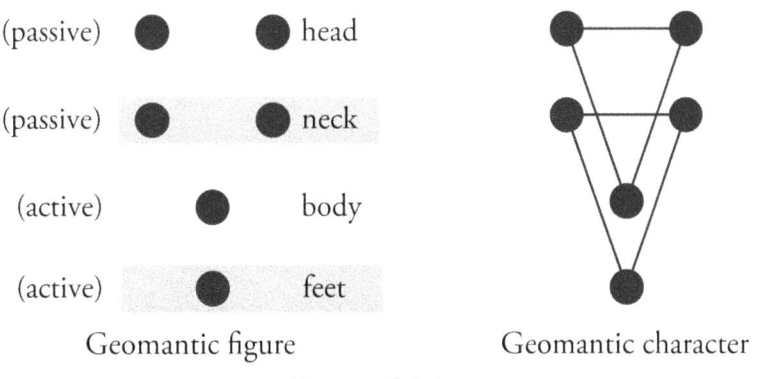

Geomantic figure   Geomantic character

Fortuna Major

Scripts and Ciphers

According to the Bible, following the confusion of tongues at the Tower of Babel, a multitude of human languages appeared. It is thought that this event preceded the beginning of civilization by some 500 years. Civilization required a quick, cheap method of writing for recording religious, legal, administrative and literary documents. This came in the form of the phonetic alphabet, papyrus or paper, a reed pen and ink.

Reed pens were first invented in Sumer, used to incise pictograms and logograms into tablets of damp clay. The Egyptians used a soft reed pen with which the ink was brushed on to papyrus to write simplified hieroglyphs. Around 300 BCE, the Greeks invented the hard reed pen with a split nib to write on papyrus and dried animal skin called parchment, enabling the development of calligraphy, meaning 'beautiful writing'.

Calligraphy led to the creation of formal scripts or book hands formed entirely of capital letters, their standard height and shape distinguished them from cursive script or handwriting with its ascenders and descenders.

As the same time as early Jewish cabala was being formulated, book hands evolved into the sacred script styles of the emerging Abrahamic religions spreading across the Middle East, Europe and Africa. Judaism, Christianity and other religions self-identified through the language and script used to write the Word of God as scripture in Holy Books. Such scripts are those found in illuminated manuscripts, produced from the 1st century CE to the establishment of letterpress printing in the 16th century.

During the Middle Ages, it became popular to write the names of God and the Angels in an ancient script such as those used by the Hebrews, Greeks and Copts or Egyptian Christians. It was believed that these scripts held great magical properties because of their antiquity.

In the 15th and 16th centuries, discovering ancient and esoteric alphabets became popular among some intellectuals and a great undertaking took place as learned men sought to find the original language, alphabet and script used by Adam in the Garden of Eden and what became of it after the Fall.

The result was the calligraphic reproduction of ancient Hebrew, Aramaic, Samaritan, Syriac and other scripts, including those attributed to Angels and the Hebrew Patriarchs, Adam, Enoch, Noah, Abraham and Moses, or a mystical personality such as Solomon or Apollonius. Renditions of these scripts and many others were published in the 16th, 17th and 18th centuries in various books known as 'Pantographia'.

In the same centuries, magicians, alchemists, hermetics and secret societies collected or invented occult scripts and ciphers. The most well-known of these were reproduced by Cornelius Agrippa in his grimoire, the Occult Philosophies. The same set of magic scripts were also listed in the Key of Solomon. In the 19th and 20th centuries, individual adepts such as Aleister Crowley and Neopagan groups have either revived or developed their own.

From the medieval era onwards, adepts, magicians and secret societies have used alphabetic ciphers and number mysticism to encode esoteric knowledge or the names of spirits in the form of sigils, recording them in grimoires or magical training books.

Most of these occult scripts are simple substitute ciphers for existing languages such as Hebrew, Greek or Latin. As such, they are more useful for their esoteric value or ritual purpose. Sigils are related but a distinct concept where a magician uses alpha-numerology to create a secret sign to invoke a spirit or manifest a desired effect.

Hebrew Scripts

Over the millennia, the Hebrew language has been written in a variety of distinct scripts, all of which descend from the Phoenician alphabet, a Semitic script adapted to write the related languages of Aramean, Moabite, Samaritan, Syriac, Nabatean and Arabic, amongst others.

The first of the Hebrew scripts, Ktav Ivri or Old Hebrew, is a variant of the Phoenician script that was the model for the ancient Israelites. It is said to be the original script of the Torah and is also thought by some to be the original script of Moses and the Ten Commandments. It is still used by Samaritan Jews to write the Torah. The oldest known inscription in Ktav Ivri is the Gezer calendar, dated to the 11th or 10th century BCE.

Hebrew and the Ktav Ivri were replaced as the common language and script of the Israelites by the closely related Aramaic language written in the Ashurit or Assyrian script during the Babylonian captivity of the 6th century BCE.

The Jerusalem Talmud quotes: *"The Israelites took for themselves square calligraphy"* and that the letters *"came with the Israelites from Ashur (Assyria)."*

Ktav Ashurit, meaning 'written Assyrian', is the traditional Hebrew name for the Hebrew alphabet. Also called the 'square script', the names Ashurit and square script are used to distinguish it from the Ktav Ivri script.

Ashurit script is a black letter calligraphic style derived from Neo-Aramaic cuneiform signs and developed by the Assyrians to write Imperial Aramaic, the 'lingua franca' or administrative, religious and business language of the Assyrian Empire, similar to that of Rome's use of Latin.

Although Aramaic replaced Hebrew as the common language of the Jews, the Hebrew language was retained by the rabbi's for religious writings.

Around 325 BCE, God instructed Ezra the scribe to create the 22 letters of the Ktav Ashurit as to His instructions, to replace the Ktav Ivri for the copying of the Torah. To downplay the historical significance of this event, its name was changed from Ashurit to Meruba meaning 'square', the name by which it is known today.

Since that time, Ktav Meruba has been the standard formal book hand of Hebrews and the model for all Hebrew typefaces.

The Torah is traditionally written in Ktav Meruba using a feather brush or quill on parchment scrolls. The Torah, Tefllin, Mezzuzot and the five Megillot can be written in any of its ceremonial variants called Ktav STA'M; which include the addition of Taggin or 'crowns', an aid to the reader's spiritual awareness of the letters of the text.

After centuries in exile, Jews have developed two primary ceremonial traditions, Ashkenzai and Sefaradi, with slight differences between them.

Ashkenazi is the name given to all Central and East European Jews. Their Meruba variant is slightly Gothic in style, reflecting its Germanic origins. Ashkenazi ceremonial script comes in two distinct forms; Ktav Ben Yosef or standard Ashkenazi, and Ari or Arizal, employed by the Chassidic or Hassidic Jews of Palestine, Syria and Iraq. The two Ashkenazi scripts differ slightly on only five or six letters.

Sephardic, also called Vellish, was employed by Sefardic or Spanish-speaking Jews living in Spain and Portugal. It is the standard script used by Mizrahim and Teimanim for writing the primary text of the Talmud.

Rashi or rabbinical script is a semi-cursive variant of Square Hebrew, used by rabbi's for writing commentaries in Jewish Holy books. In the 15th century, a Sefardic variant was adapted for letterpress printing by early printers. They named the typeface Rashi and used it to distinguish Rabbi Rashi's commentaries in the Talmud from the main text printed in Ktav Meruba. It was extensively used in Jewish writing in medieval Italy and Germany and has a similar role to that of Italic type.

Cursive Hebrew is the informal, handwritten script used in schools, in business and for personal correspondence. Over the centuries, various localized variants have developed from Square Hebrew, the modern variant is descended from the Ashkenzai or Polish/German form.

אבגדהוזחטיכלמנסעפצקרשת
T Sh R Q Tz P O S N M L K I Th Ch Z V H D G B A

Ktav Ivri - Old Hebrew - 900 BCE

T Sh R Q Tz P O S N M L K I Th Ch Z V He D G B A

Samaritan - 500 BCE

T Sh R Q SS P O S N M L K Y Th Ch Z W H D G B A

Early Aramaic - 900 BCE

אבגדהוזחטילמנסעכצקרשת
T Sh R Q Tz P O S N M L K I Th Ch Z V He D G B A

Old Imperial Aramaic - 600 BCE

T Sh R Q Tz P O S N M L K I Th Ch Z V He D G B A

Late Imperial Aramaic - 300 BCE

אבגדהוזחטיכלמנסעפצקרשת
ך ם ן ף ץ
T Sh R Q Tz P O S N M L K I Th Ch Z V He D G B A

Ktav Ashurit - Assyrian writing / Ktav Meruba - Square script with final characters

אבגדהוזחטיככלמנסעפצקרשת
T Sh R Q Tz P O S N M L K I Th Ch V He D G B A

Ashkenzai (German) - Ktav Ben Yosef with Taggin (crowns)

אבגדהוזחטיכךלמםנןסעפףצץקרשת
T Sh R Q Tz P O S N M L K I Th Ch Z V He D G B A

Sefaradi / Vellish (Spanish) - script and typeface

אבגדהוזחטיכךלמםנןסעפףצקרשת
T Sh R Q Tz P O S N M L K I Th Ch Z V He D G B A

Rashi typeface - 15th century

T Sh R Q Tz P O S N M L K I Th Ch Z V He D G B A

Modern Hebrew cursive - 20th century

Syriac and Persian Scripts

Syriac is a Semitic language closely related to Hebrew, Moabite, Samaritan and Aramaic. The Syriac dialect hails from Edessa (Urfa, Northwest Turkey) and became an important literary language around the 3rd century CE.

An offshoot of old cursive Aramaic script, the calligraphic stylings of the letters of Syriac script are formed by a split-reed pen or a feather dipped in ink and written on parchment of vellum, in the Ashurit or Assyrian script style. There were several varieties of Syriac script, all of which were superseded by Arabic in the 14th century.

Some scholars are of the opinion that Syriac calligraphy antecedes that of other peoples of the world and that the Syrians taught mankind the early method of writing, from which the Phoenicians and other nations borrowed their scripts.

A recent archeological find suggests the Syrians may have invented the alphabet after an artefact, dating from 2500 BCE was discovered inscribed with alphabetic script. Others think it was the Arameans who may have been the inventors, as they lived in Syria around the same time.

The oldest of the Aramaic derived Syriac scripts dates to 50 CE. By the Christian era, a distinctive calligraphic form called Estrangela, 'rounded' appeared in the cultural center of Edessa. It functioned as the script of Syrian Christians and was used exclusively from the 1st century CE till the 14th century and is considered the source of Arabic Kufic script.

In 489 CE, a schism occurred in the Syrian Christian church between the followers of Jacob of Edessa and Nestorius of Persia. This not only split the church but started the process of splitting the Estrangla script in two variants, western and eastern.

The western variant called Serto (linear, simple) emerged during the 8th century CE to function as the religious script of the western Syrian church founded by Jacob of Edessa, and is often referred to as Jacobite script. It was a slightly more cursive version of Estrangla and became the model for the Arabic Nashki script used to write the Islamic scriptures of the Quran.

From the 6th century CE onwards the Chaldean or eastern variant of Estrangela called Mankhavi, evolved more slowly out of Estrangla, only showing a slightly distinct look by the 12th century. It was a conservative script employed in Persia by the Assyrian Orthodox Church and the followers of the early Christian Nestorius. The Nestorian script spread as far as central Asia where it was written vertically in Syriac-Chinese inscriptions. Nestorianism died out in 13th to 14th century.

As Syriac was the liturgical language of Syrian Christianity it was used to write the liturgical dialects of Manichaean. The Manichaeans were a major religious sect living in Iran. They believed in a basis of doctrine on which to unite the different sects of the Christian church and the various religions of the world. They developed their late Aramaic variant in the 3rd c. CE, to write Persian and East Turkic, following their expulsion from Iraq.

Syriac script was also employed by several new, now extinct Gnostic faiths including Mandaean. Mandaean script developed during the 7th century CE, in the Basra region of Iraq. Mandaean means 'knowledge' in Arabic and Mandaenism is the only surviving Gnostic religion. Originally founded in Palestine, these followers of John the Baptists called Jesus a false prophet. They left Jerusalem in 70 CE and moved to Babylon before arriving Iraq in 636. In Iraq they differed with Islam, calling Mohammed the "demon Bizbat". Its remaining followers live in southern Iraq and southwest Iran.

From the 3rd century BCE to the 9th century CE, the Late Aramaic derived, Pahlavi script was used to write Middle Persian, the religious language of Zoroastrianism. Its most common form was Book Pahlavi used to write the Avesta, the Holy Book of Zoroasterism.

Avestan script was created in the 3rd century CE for recording the Avesta hymns composed by Zoroaster / Zarathustra in the Old Persian or Gathic language in the 6th century BCE. It is derived from the older Pahlavi script and shows a Greek influence. Following the Islamic conquest of Persia, Avesta was replaced by Arabic script, while Zoroastrians continued to write their scriptures in Pahlavi for centuries after.

Oldest form of Assyrian Script (Aramaic)

| A | B | G | D | H | V | Z | Ch | Th | I | K | L | M | N | S | O | P | Tz | Q | R | Sh | T |

Old Syriac Script

| A | B | G | D | H | V | Z | Ch | Th | I | K | L | M | N | S | P | Tz | Q | R | Sh | T |

Estrangela (Round)

| A | B | G | D | H | V | Z | Ch | Th | I | L | K | M | H | N | S | P | Tz | Q | R | Sh | T |

Western Estrangela / Serto – Syrian Christian – 100 CE

| A | B | G | D | H | V | Z | H | Th | Y | K | L | M | H | S | O | P | Z | Q | R | Sh | T |

Eastern Estrangela / Magnkhaya – Nestorian Christian – 200 CE

| A | B | G | D | H | V | Z | H | Th | Y | K | L | M | H | S | O | P | Z | Q | R | Sh | T |

Manichean (Christian)

| A | B | G | Gh | D | He | H | Z | W | Th | Y | K | L | Dh | M | N | Se | O | P | Sa | J | Q | R | Sh | T |

Mandaean (Gnostic)

| A | B | G | D | H | W | Z | Th | Y | K | L | M | N | S | E | F | SS | Q | R | Sh | T |

Syriac Scripts

Book Pahlavi

| A | B | G/D/Y | H | R | V/N/O | Z | K | L | M/Q | S | P | Tz | Sh | T |

Avestan

a	aa	ao	aao	an	aen	ae	aee	e	ee	o	oo	i	ii	u	uu	ka	xa	xya	xva
ga	gya	gha	ca	ja	ta	tha	da	dha	tta	pa	fa	ba	wa	nga	ngya	ngva
na	nya	nna	ma	mya	yya	ya	va	ra	sa	za	sha	zha	shya	shha	ha

Persian Zoroastrian scripts

Arabic and Ethiopian Scripts

By 600 CE, Arabic script had evolved out of the late Aramaic-derived Nabatean script into the classic form still used today. With the rise of Islam, Arabic script was used to write the Quran, the Holy Book of Islam, in many languages.

The development of Arabic calligraphy and Islamic religious scripts can be traced back to the 9th century, beginning with the angular, stone-carved, Kufic script. Kufic was replaced by the six cursive scripts of the Sitta, invented in the 10th century by Abu Ali Muhammad ibn Muqlah, a visor in Baghdad. The six scripts are Thuluth, Naskhi, Rayhani, Muhaqqaq, Tauqi and Riqa. Four of which are or have been used to write the Quran.

These scripts were further perfected by Yaqut al-Musta'simi (died 1298) at the court of Baghdad and assigned to different kinds of writing; Riqa for correspondence, Tauqi for official documents, Muhaqqaq for poetry, Thuluth for instruction and practice, Rayhani for Qur'an copies, and Naskhi for commentaries of the Qur'an. Later, four more scripts, Ghubar, Tumar, Ta'liq and Nasta'liq were included.

Kufic script takes its name from the city of Kufah in southern Iraq, where it was first developed as a monumental form for stone inscriptions. This angular script was adapted for writing religious texts because of its formality, as it is drawn as opposed to written. Kufic was replaced by Muhaqqaq and Rayhani script for writing the Quran in the 10th century CE, but retained for decorative purposes, having variants called 'flowering' and 'geometric'.

Also known as the Mecca-Medina script, Naskhi is derived from the Arabic word 'nasakha', meaning 'to copy' or 'translate'. A simple cursive script, it is one of the Sitta, developed in the 10th century for writing commentaries on the Quran. It was reformed in the 13th century, giving the script its present-day form, and replaced Rihani in the 17th century as the script for Quran copies.

Muhaqqaq means 'fully realized' or 'strongly expressed'. First developed in the 10th century and refined in the 13th century, it was used for writing architectural inscriptions and fine, large copies of the Quran, often in conjunction with the Rayhani script. It was replaced by the Thuluth script in the 11th century, but is still used for writing 'Bismillah'.

Thuluth means 'one third' and refers to being one-third the pen size used to write a larger script called Tumar. Thuluth is monumental in style. Developed in the 10th century to write architectural inscriptions and refined in the 13th century, it replaced Muhaqqaq for large copies of the Quran, where it is used in conjunction with the Naskhi script.

Khatt'i Reagan (Rayhani/Rihani script) means 'basil' or 'having fragrance'. Developed in the 10th century and used in conjunction with Muhaqqaq for writing copies of the Quran, it was a smaller version of the Muhaqqaq script. It was replaced by the Naskhi script for copies of the Quran in the 11th century and refined in the 13th century.

Mahgrib is an Arabic word that means 'western'. This form of Arabic script was developed in the 10th century by Muslims living in North Africa and in Spain, where it is called the 'Andalusian script'. It is the most geographically limited of Islamic scripts, never extending beyond the Maghreb (Morocco, Tunisia and Algeria). A less rigid version of Kufic, it is used to write copies of the Qur'an as well as religious, scientific and legal texts.

Around 500 BCE, the South Semitic script evolved to write the languages of southern Arabia. Arabian settlers took the South Semitic-derived Sabaic script to Ethiopia, where it was used to write the Ge'ez language and evolved into Old Ethiopic.

Ge'ez is no longer used for day to day purposes, but remains the liturgical language of the Orthodox and Catholic Churches of Ethiopia and Eritrea. The script used to write these Cushite languages is called Fidal, meaning 'script', 'alphabet', 'letter' or 'character'. At first, this left to right writing system represented only consonants. Vowel indication started to appear in the 4th century CE under the influence of Christianity. Under the influence of Indian traders, it developed in to an Abugida or alpha-syllabic writing system, used to write Amharic, the lingua franca of Ethiopia, the official working language of the Ethiopian government and considered a Holy language by Rastafarians.

Late Aramaic - 200 CE

| T | Sh | R | Q | Tz | P | O | S | N | M | L | K | I | Th | Ch | Z | V | H | D | G | B | A |

Nabatean - 400 CE

| T | Sh | R | Q | SS | P | O | S | N | M | L | K | Y | Th | Kh | Z | W | H | D | G | B | A |

Early Arabic - 600 CE

| T | Sh | R | Q | SS | P | O | S | N | M | L | K | Y | Th | Kh | Z | W | H | D | G | B | A |

Classic Kufic (independent letterforms)

| S | N | M | L | C | I | T | Ch | Z | V | He | D | G | B | A |

| La | Gc | Thz | Dz | Dh | Ch | Th | Tz | Sc | R | K | Ts | Ph | HH |

Naskhi (independent letterforms)

| S | N | M | L | K | I/Y | T | Ch | Z | W | He | D | J | B | A |

| Gh | Dha | D | Dh | Kh | Th | Tz | Sh | R | Q | Sa | F | O |

Muhaqqaq

Thuluth

Rayhani / Rihani

Mahgrib script (N. Africa, Spain)

Sitta scripts used to write the Qur'an

Fidal / Amharic (Ethiopic Christianity) - 600 CE

| h | l | hh | m | sz | r | s | q | b | t | kh | n | a | k | w | o | z | y | d | g | th | ph | ts | tz | f | p |

Uncial Scripts

Also known as Late Roman or Early Christian letters, uncial, meaning 'one inch' or 'one twelfth', which refers to the height of the letters, is a majuscule book hand used as a main text script, especially in high-grade Christian books, and thereafter as a display script.

Originally derived from handwritten capitals, uncial was originally developed by Greek and Roman scribes. The earliest versions date from the late 1st and early 2nd centuries CE and it was in common use between the 4th and 8th centuries.

In Rome, uncial letter forms quickly replaced the use of display capitals because they were more elegant and easier and quicker to write than the traditional majuscule styles of Rustica and Capitalis Quadrata or Square Capitals.

Uncial was first used to write everything that needed recording before Early Christians employed it as a formal script or book hand, helping them to form a religious identity. Around 400 CE, the Romans created the half-uncial script, which can be considered a prototype for an alphabet consisting purely of small letters or minuscules.

Uncial was extremely widespread, used in Classical Greece, Rome, Byzantium and Egypt, and medieval Italy, France, Spain, Britain and Ireland.

As the script evolved over the centuries, the characters became more complex and stylized around 600 CE. It is the script used by Italian luxury Bible manuscripts in the 6th and 7th centuries and for insular manuscripts under Italian influence, as at the Monastery of Jarrow, Northumberland.

The insular form of uncial was used in Ireland and Britain. The script was brought to southern England from Rome by the missionary, Saint Augustine, in 597; after which, southern English insular scripts were developed in places such as Canterbury. As these scripts moved northward, they came under the influence of the insular majuscule, which they tried to emulate and outshine.

Natural uncial is the term given to those scripts based on the natural hand movements with which uncial is written. Artificial uncial is a script whose letter forms are created using more unnatural hand movements to create the letter forms.

Uncials were still used, particularly for copying the Bible, until around the 10th century outside of Ireland, when they were replaced by the Carolingian and the Gothic minuscule scripts between the 8th and 12th centuries.

Following the death of Christ, Egyptian Christians or Copts (Copt being the Arab name for Egypt) adapted the Greek uncial script to write the Gospels in the Egyptian language.

The Coptic script adapted the entire Greek alphabet and supplemented it with six additional letters derived from the Egyptian Demotic script, giving a total of 32 letters to the Coptic alphabet.

In early medieval times, 600 CE, the Semitic letter order and the Coptic letters of Egyptian Christians were combined to form the Old Nubian script. As a writing system, Coptic script died out in the 14th century, replaced by Arabic and Latin.

The Gothic language was spoken in East Germany and Bulgaria and originally written in rune script before it was given a Christian script by Bishop Ulfilas or Wulfila in the 4th century CE. Largely derived from the Greek alphabet, it contains 6 Latin letters and 2 of runic origin, giving 25 letters in all. Ulfilas invented it to translate the Gospels and other parts of the New Testament.

By the 6th century, the language was in decline, following defeats by the Franks. The script was used in Crimea up until the 17th century, when it was replaced by the Cyrillic alphabet

In 16th century Europe, uncial script was replaced as a book hand by the Romanized majuscule and minuscule letters of the Renaissance and the Roman typefaces of early Italian printers.

The Irish insular uncial remained in the standard script used to write the Irish language until the middle of the 20th century; by which time, all uncial scripts had been replaced with Romanized letter forms of the dual alphabet.

ABCDEFGHIJKLMNOPQRSTUVWXYZ
Capitalis Rustica - 100 CE

ABCDEFGHIJKLMNOPQRSTUVWXYZ
Capitalis Quadrata (Square Capital) - 100 CE

λ ɑ c d E F a h i L M N o ſ a ſ ſ τ ᴗ x
Old Roman cursive (cursive majuscule / handwriting) - 1st century CE - 3rd century CE

ΑΒΓΔΕΖΗΘΙΚΛΜΝΞΟΠΡϹΤΥΦΧΨω
Greek uncial - 100 CE

ABCDEFGHIJKLMNOPQRSTUVWXYZ
Littera Uncia / Roman uncial - 300 CE

Ⲁ	Ⲃ	Ⲅ	Ⲇ	Ⲉ	Ⳅ	Ⲋ	Ⲏ	Ⲡ	Ⲣ	Ⲥ	Ⲧ	Ⲩ	Ⲫ	Ⲭ	Ⲯ
ⲁ	ⲃ	ⲅ	ⲇ	ⲉ	ⳅ	ⲍ	ⲏ	ⲡ	ⲣ	ⲥ	ⲧ	ⲩ	ⲫ	ⲭ	ⲯ
A	B,V	G	D	E	Ǝ	Dz	Ei	P	R	S	T	U	Ph	Kh	PS

Ⲑ	Ⲓ	Ⲕ	Ⲗ	Ⲙ	Ⲛ	Ⲝ	Ⲟ	Ⲱ	Ϣ	Ϥ	Ϧ	Ϩ	Ϫ	Ϭ	Ϯ
ⲑ	ⲓ	ⲕ	ⲗ	ⲙ	ⲛ	ⲝ	ⲟ	ⲱ	ϣ	ϥ	ϧ	ϩ	ϫ	ϭ	ϯ
Th	I	K	L	M	N	Ks	O	OO	S	F	X	H	Dz	Ts	Ti

Egyptian uncial / Coptic - 400 CE

ⲁ	ⲃ	ⲅ	ⲇ	ⲉ	ⲏ	ⲍ	ⲑ	ⲓ	ⲕ	ⲗ	ⲙ	ⲛ	ⲟ	ⲟⲩ
A	B	G	D	E	H	I	Th	Y	K	L	M	N	O	U

ⲡ	ⲣ	ⲥ	ⲧ	ⲓ	ⲫ	ⲭ	ⲯ	ⲱ	ϣ	ϩ	ⳟ	ⳝ	ⳡ
P	R	S	T	I	Ph	Ch	Ps	O	S	H	G	N	W

Old Nubian uncial / Coptic - 500 CE

ABCDEFGHIJKLMNOPQRSTUVWXYZ
Insular / Artificial uncial (Britain) - 500 CE

ABCDEFGHIJKLMNOPQRSTUVWXYZ
Natural uncial (Luxeuil, France) - 600 CE

Ⰰ	Ⰱ	Ⰳ	Ⰴ	Ⰵ	Ⰶ	Ⰷ	Ⰸ	Ⰹ	Ⰺ	Ⰻ	Ⰼ	Ⰽ	Ⰾ	Ⰿ	Ⱀ	Ⱁ	Ⱂ	Ⱃ	Ⱄ	Ⱅ	Ⱆ	Ⱇ	Ⱈ	Ⱉ
A	B	G	D	E	Q	Z	H	Th	I	K	L	M	N	Ng	U	P	R	S	T	V	F	Ks	W	O

Gothic uncial - 900 CE

ΑΒΓΔΕΖΗΘΙΚΛΜΝΞΟΠΡϹΤΥΦΧΨШΘ
Greek uncial - 1200 CE

Roman Letters

The Roman Church was founded by St. Peter when he arrived in Rome in 50 CE. The Romans did not convert to Christianity until 380 CE, when it became the official religion of the empire. Since its split from the early Christian Church and its development into Roman Catholicism, the religion has given birth to many breakaway churches that have all used the Latin language and Roman letters to represent their Christian beliefs.

The Roman-based alphabets of European Christians are unique in religious and non-religious writing, stemming from the fact that they are 'dual' alphabet made up of two alphabetic scripts. One script representing the capital, majuscule or uppercase letters. The other representing the small, minuscule or lowercase letters. Both scripts are derived from ancient Roman models.

The Romans took their inspiration for their stone-carved letters from the Greeks. From a calligraphic point of view, the Greeks applied a geometric structure and order to the uneven Phoenician letters. The written form of Greek had a visual order and balance as the letters move along a baseline in an even repetition of form and space.

Monumental Greek capitals are symmetrical geometric constructions, stone-carvers took imaginative liberties with letterform design while maintaining the basic structure. The letters E and M are based on squares, A is constructed from an equilateral triangle and O is a near perfect circle. The letters and their component strokes became somewhat standardized because of a system of horizontal, vertical, curved and diagonal strokes with the ends of the letter strokes square cut. They became the model for sans serif typefaces of printers.

The carved letter forms of the Imperial Roman Capital, or Capitalis Monumentalis, date back to the 1st century BCE when they were used extensively; chiseled into stone and marble, inscribed on tombs, monuments and arches. In the first century CE, under the patronage of the Emperor Trajan, the Imperial Roman capital reached a peak of stylized perfection with the carved letter forms on Trajan's column in Rome.

Romans painted their capital letters onto a stone surface with a brush and then cut them out with a chisel, making them cursive or hand written as opposed to a geometric in structure. The Romans also added serifs, to improve legibility from a distance. They became the source of serif capitals used by printers.

Apart from monumental capitals and uncial majuscules, the Romans employed two forms of display capital, Rustica and Capitalsi Quadrata, as book hands for writing manuscripts.

From 400 CE onwards, Roman scribes developed the half-uncial script from the uncial script to save time and money in the copying of bibles and other texts. The half-uncial became the model for the minuscule or lowercase letters, resulting in the creation of the Carolingian minuscule around 800 CE, the model for today's lowercase letters.

Between the 10th and 15th centuries, the compact Gothic blackletter scripts, Textura, Rotunda and Fractur, producing very heavy, dense pages of text, were employed by Catholics and Protestants to save even more time and materials in copying bibles.

In the last years of the 14th century, Humanist scribes of the Italian Renaissance began experimenting with a new script as a cleaner alternative to the plethora of Gothic scripts that existed at that time. At the beginning of the 16th century, Poggio Pracciolini created a new script, known as Littera Antiqua, in imitation of the Carolingian minuscule and its associated display majuscule script, the Square Roman capital, to create the basis of the Romanized dual alphabet of capital and lowercase letters of today.

This style proved popular with the first Italian printers of the late 15th century and although both Humanist and Gothic typefaces were used continuously until the 20th century, Roman type became the standard typestyle in the West for printing all forms of texts, religious and secular.

The Times New Roman typeface was created for the 'The Times' newspaper in the 1920s and its capitals are based on the letter forms incised on Trajan's column. The modern Greek alphabet is also written and printed as a dual alphabet of Romanized letters.

ΑΒΓΔΕΖΗΘΙΚΛΜΝΞΟΠϹΡϹΤΥΦΧϮΩ
A B G D E Z H Th I K L M N X O P Q R S T U Ph Kh Ps O

Classic Greek monumental capitals (Geometric)

ABCDEFGHIJKLMNOPQRSTUVWXYZ

Roman Capitalis Monumentalis - 100 CE (Cursive)

abcdefʒhijklmnopqrv tuvwxyz

New Roman cursive (business handwriting) - 3rd - 5th centuries CE

abcdefghijklmnopqrstuvwxyz

Roman Half-Uncial - 350 CE

abcdefghijklmnopqrstuvwxyz

Insular Half-Uncial (Celtic church) - 500 CE

abcdefghijklmnopqrstuvwxyz

Caroliangian Minuscule (Holy Roman Church) - 800 CE

abcdefghijklmnopqrstuvwxyz

Gothic Blackletter / Textura (Catholic / Protestant) - 1200 CE

Minuscule scripts - lower case

ABCDEFGHIJKLMNOPQRSTUVWXYZ
abcdefghijklmnopqrstuvwxyz

Lettera Antiqua - majuscules and minuscules (all denominations) - 1400 CE

ABCDEFGHIJKLMNOPQRSTUVWXYZ
abcdefghijklmnopqrstuvwxyz

Times New Roman typeface

Α Β Γ Δ Ε Ζ Η Θ Ι Κ Λ Μ Ν Ξ Ο Π Ρ Σ Τ Υ Φ Χ Ψ Ω
α β γ δ ε ζ η θ ι κ λ μ ν ξ ο π ρ σ τ υ φ χ ψ ω
A B G D E Z H Th I K L M N Kh O P R S T U Phi X Ps OO

Modern Greek dual alphabet and Romanized typeface

Roman and Greek Christian scripts

Cyrillic Scripts

The Cyrillic script is the book hand of the Russian Orthodox Church, an umbrella term used to describe the Eastern Orthodox Christian churches of the Balkans, Eastern Europe and Russia, as opposed to the Greek Orthodox and Roman Christian churches in western Europe.

Between the 4th and 7th centuries CE, eastern Europe was still largely untouched by Christianity and Roman and Greek churches spread across eastern Europe bringing alphabetic writing with them. At this time, East German, Bulgarian and Slavic speaking people, either used a form of runic script or had no alphabets of their own and their language was ill-suited to the unaltered adaptation of Roman or Greek scripts.

Christian missionaries created the new alphabets and scripts needed for the transliteration of the Bible and other religious works into east European languages. The Croats and Poles converted to Roman Catholicism, receiving a Roman script derived from that of the Latin alphabet. The Goths, Bulgarians, Serbs and Russians converted to Orthodoxy and received an Uncial style script based on the Greek alphabet.

The first script of any Slavic language, Glagolitic, was created in the 9th century for the translation of the Bible into Old Bulgarian. Its name comes from its 3rd letter 'glagol' or "word". Its invention is attributed to the Slav apostle Konstantin, who was later known as St Cyrllus (d. 869), the inventor of the Cyrillic alphabet and script.

Glagolitic was used for a relatively short period of time, replaced in the 12th century by the Cyrillic script that became the literary standard called Old Church Slavonic.

Also known as Asbuku, after its first two letters, the Cyrillic alphabet is used by Slavic and non-Slavic speaking people living mainly in the Russian federation. Said to have been created by the 9th century Slav apostles, Saint Cyrillus and his brother Methodius, under the authority of Emperor Michael III, or it may have been invented by St Kliment of Ohrid.

Most of the letters of the Cyrillic script are derived from the Greek uncial script. Five more are taken from the Glagolitic alphabet. In 1708, under the Russian Tsar, Peter the Great, the Cyrillic script was simplified and the letter forms romanised. In 1917-18 four letters were eliminated under Communist writing reforms.

In modern times Cyrillic is used to write Belorussian, Bulgarian, Ukrainian, Russian and other non-Slavic languages of the ex-Soviet Union including Romanian, Moldovian, Kazakhstani, Turkmenistani, Uzbekistani and Mongolian. It is also used by various Inuit and Eskimo tribes living in the Russian Arctic circle.

In many cases, additional letters are used, adaptations of standard Cyrillic letters or taken from the Greek and Latin alphabets. Today, the Cyrillic script is mostly associated with the anti-religious, political ideology of Soviet Communism.

A	B	V	G	D	E	Z	Dz	Z	I	I	D,Y	K	L

M	N	O	P	R	S	T	U	F	X	O	St	Ts

Ts	S	O,E	U	I	Ye, Ya	Yu	O	E	Yo	Ye	Th	OO

Glagolitic / Old Bulgarian - 600 CE

А	Б	В	Г	Д	Є	Ж	Ѕ	Z	И	І	К	Л	М	Н	О
A	B,P	V,F	G,K	D	E	Sh	Zh	Z	I	I	K	L	M	N	O

П	Р	С	Т	У	Ф	Х	Ц	Ч	Ѡ	Щ	Ы	З	Ю	Я	Ѳ	V
P	R	S	T	OO	F	Kh	Ts	Ch	Sh	Shch	Y	E	Yu	Ya	F	Y/V

Old Slavonic / Cyrillic (uncial) - 850 CE

А	Б	В	Г	Д	Е	Ж	З	И	К	Л	М	Н	О	П	Р	С
A	B,P	V,F	G,K	D	E	Sh,Zh	Z	I	K	L	M	N	O	P	R	S

Т	У	Ф	Х	Ц	Ч	Ш	Щ	Ъ	Ы	Э	Ю	Я	Ѳ	V
T	OO	F	Kh	Ts	Ch	Sh	Shch	I	Y	Ye	E	Yu	Ya	F	Y,V

Modern Romanized Cyrillic typeface - 1900 CE

Eastern Orthodox Christian scripts - Slavic

Chaldean Scripts

During the Middle Ages, it became popular to write the names of God and the Angels in an ancient script such as Hebrew, Greek or Egyptian. It was believed that these scripts held great magical properties because of their antiquity.

In the 15th and 16th centuries, discovering ancient and exotic alphabets became popular among some European intellectuals, including Dr. John Dee, and a great undertaking took place as learned men sought to find the original language, alphabet and script used by Adam in the Garden of Eden before the Fall.

They conceived that the original alphabet from which all others, ancient and modern, have been derived are no more than three.

1. The Old Syrian (Assyrian/Ashurit (Chaldean)), first divine alphabet taught by God the Almighty to Adam.
2. The Angelic/Celestial alphabet, in which the books that Seth received from Heaven were written.
3. The Alphabet of Enoch, brought down to Earth by the Archangel Gabriel.

Called Chaldean at the time, the Assyrian or Ashurit script was thought to be the script used to write the Adamic language, a theoretical language believed to be the first language and the one that shaped Creation. According to Jewish and some Christian traditions, the Adamic language is either the language spoken by God to address Adam or the language invented by Adam with which he named all things.

Adam is said to have lost the language upon the Fall from Paradise and created a form of proto-Hebrew based on his vague memory of Adamic. It was the universal language of man until the confusion of tongues at the Tower of Babel.

It is also said that the original Adamic language was communicated by the Archangel Raphael to Adam, who used it to compose Psalms after his expulsion from the Garden of Eden. Some say it was used by Moses and the prophets who were forbidden to divulge it to mortal man.

Following the confusion of tongues, all the various human languages were developed, including an even more modified version of Adamic that we call Biblical Hebrew. The Adamic language was preserved by Heber and his son, Pelag, and passed on to Abraham as Hebrew.

This version of events became the standard account in medieval literature, such as those of the legendary Scythian king, Fenius Farsa, who appears in different versions of Irish mythology.

In one myth, Fenius was said to be one of the seventy-two chieftains who built Nimrod's Tower of Babel, but travelled to Scythia after it collapsed.

Another myth recalls that he travelled from Scythia to the plains of Shinar (Sumer) with a retinue of seventy-two scholars to study the confused languages at Nimrod's tower. Finding that the speakers had already dispersed, he sent his scholars to study them, while he stayed at the tower to coordinate the effort. There he is said to have discovered Greek, Hebrew and Latin. After ten years, he created Goidelic as the perfect writing system for his language.

Renaissance scholars considered the Adamic language to be an ancient form of Hebrew and therefore written in the Hebrew Square script also called Ashurit or Assyrian by the Hebrews and Chaldean by medieval and Renaissance scholars.

In antiquity, Chaldea was used by the Hebrews and the Greeks to name those peoples of southwestern Mesopotamia. Greek and Hebrew sources also used it to describe the Assyrian (Syrian) language, and it became an alternative ethnic term for Assyrian-speaking people writing in Aramaic in northwestern Mesopotamia, before and after the advent of Christianity. The most famous Chaldean is the Hebrew Patriarch Abraham, the high priest of the city, known as Ur of Chaldea in the Bible.

The Chaldeans were considered the wisest men of their times, being well acquainted with every science and art, as it was the Chaldeans who first cultivated them. They founded a dynasty that ruled over Babylon for a short period between the 6th and 7th centuries BCE. Following the collapse of the Babylonian Empire, they moved and eventually settled in Northern Iraq, neighbours of the Kurds.

The Roman historian, Pliny, supposed the Assyrian letters were prior to any record of history, and of these he indelibly meant Chaldean. It should seem most probable that the language used by the antediluvian Patriarchs bore the greatest analogy to this, especially if it is universally allowed that they inhabited that part of the globe, whence many have thought the Chaldeans to have been prior to the Samaritans and Hebrews.

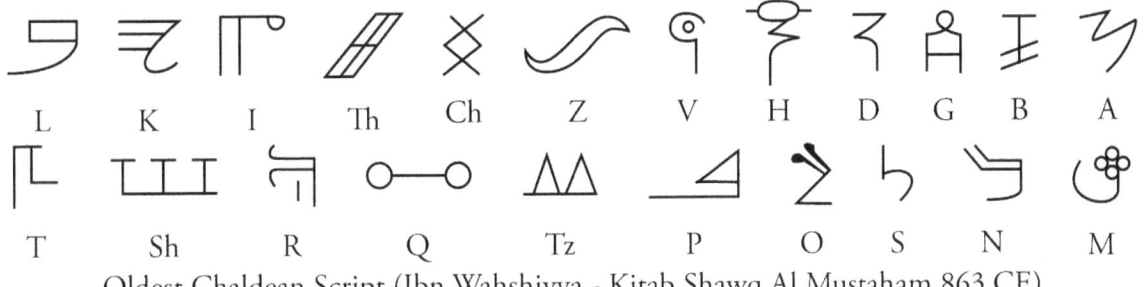
Oldest Chaldean Script (Ibn Wahshiyya - Kitab Shawq Al Mustaham 863 CE)

Chaldean 13 - Old Chaldean, Canaanite (Bagadet, Mesopotamian tribe of Turkey)

Chaldean 14 - Judaic (used during Babylonian captivity)

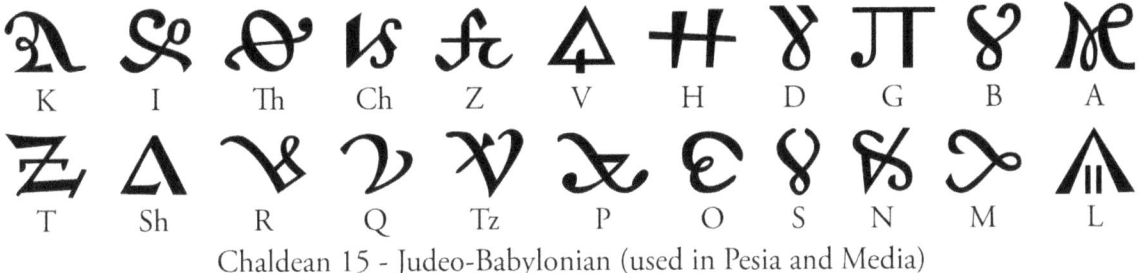
Chaldean 15 - Judeo-Babylonian (used in Pesia and Media)

Chaldean 2 - Adamic / Mosiac

Chaldean 12 - Moses (parent of all Chaldean scripts)

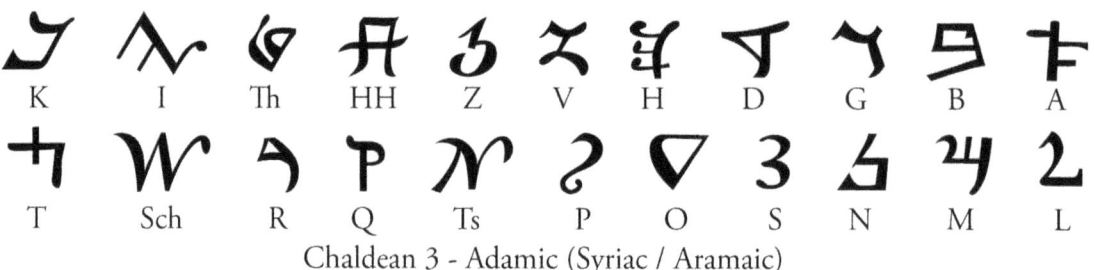
Chaldean 3 - Adamic (Syriac / Aramaic)

Chaldean 5 - Noah (Aramaic)

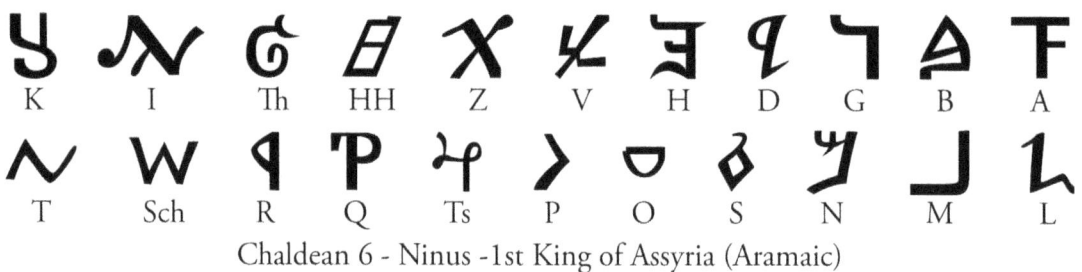
Chaldean 6 - Ninus -1st King of Assyria (Aramaic)

Chaldean 7 - Abraham (Aramaic)

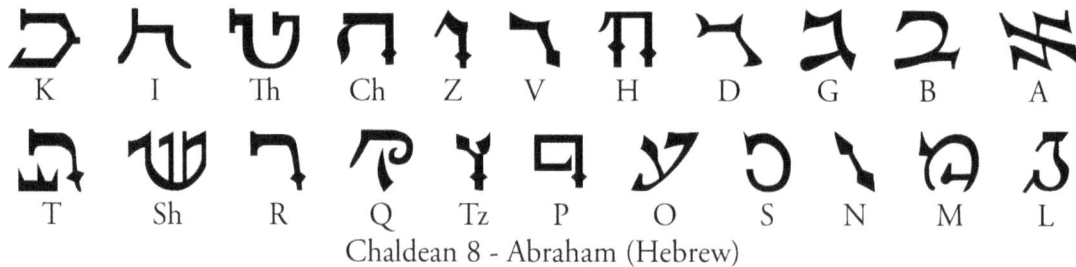
Chaldean 8 - Abraham (Hebrew)

Chaldean 11- Moses (Phoenician)

Greek

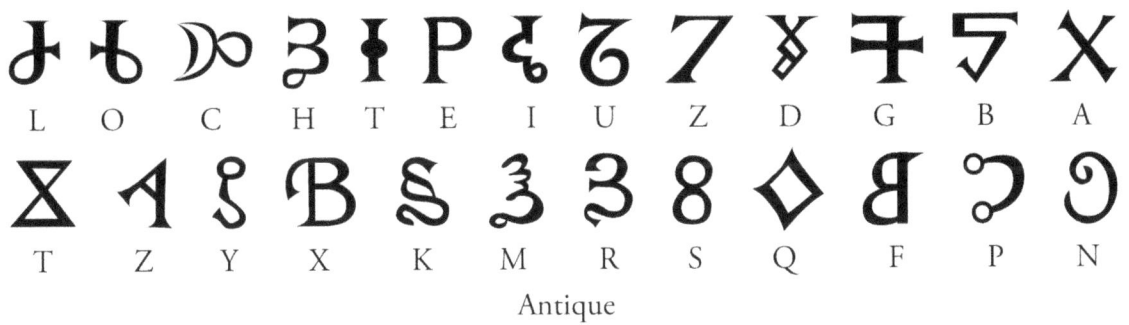

Antique

Edmund Fry's Pantographia 1788

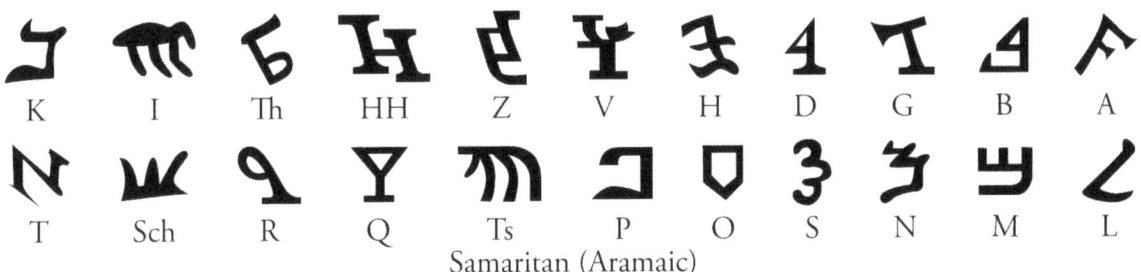

Samaritan (Aramaic)

Solomon

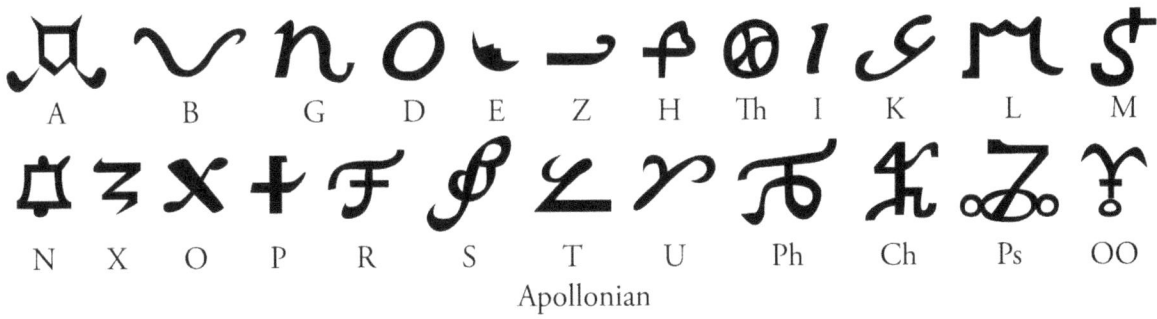

Apollonian

Chaldean Scripts

Angelic/Celestial Scripts

Angelic or Celestial writing was first revealed to mankind by Angels, specifically the Watchers, and mankind used these letters in the Garden of Eden. Angels prefer to communicate with mankind by writing and this has produced a subcategory of occult scripts referred to as Angelic or Celestial.

In cabala, each Hebrew letter is a living Angel that expresses God's voice in written form. They shape the stars that form the shapes that represent those letters. Each Angel's true name must be written in Celestial sigils to truly capture their essence.

The letterforms of Angelic script are derived from Celestial sigils or Charakteres, an ancient writing which Moses and the prophets used and were forbidden to divulge to the uninitiated. They appear in the Sefer Raziel, Jewish magical manuscripts, and were used by the Coptic Church in Late Antiquity, 100–500 CE, employed for writing the names of Angels.

These quasi-alphabetical signs are formed of strokes ending in circles. Also called 'ring letters', they are known to be inspired by the linking of shapes that are to be found in the constellations of the fixed stars of the northern and southern hemisphere's, from where they get the name Celestial. The star maps they are taken from were published in the 15th century by Graffarel.

Charakteres are not a Jewish invention, they came into existence sometime around the 2nd and 3rd centuries, probably originating from the ancient Greco-Egyptian occult tradition. They do not have a phonetic value, they are purely visual symbols, incomprehensible to humans. They were used to summon the help of supernatural beings by talking or rather writing to them in their own language, which is why they are referred to as Angelic.

Charakteres are also used in the making of charms and amulets used to gain favour; for example, by writing the charakteres or 'hatonet' on the right hand, then wiping them with olive oil and anointing the face with them.

Celestial scripts were created and employed by cabalist astrologers to express their mystical knowledge, used as ciphers for Hebrew to write the names of God and Angels on seals, pentacles and talismans.

Various versions of the script were reproduced in a number of grimoires and polygraphia. Bartolozzi's Bibliotheca Magna Rabbinica lists 7 celestial scripts, including the Celestial and Malachim, both published by Agrippa and both listed in the Key of Solomon.

Other Celestial scripts listed by Agrippa and the Key of Solomon include the 'Scriptura Transitus Fluvi' or 'Passing the River script', and the 'Writing of the Magi'.

More scripts appear in James Bonaventura Hepburn's early 17th century treatise, 'Virga Aurea', which contains seventy secret or ancient alphabets and includes Chaldean variants whose black letter forms are influenced by the Assyrian/Ashurit script.

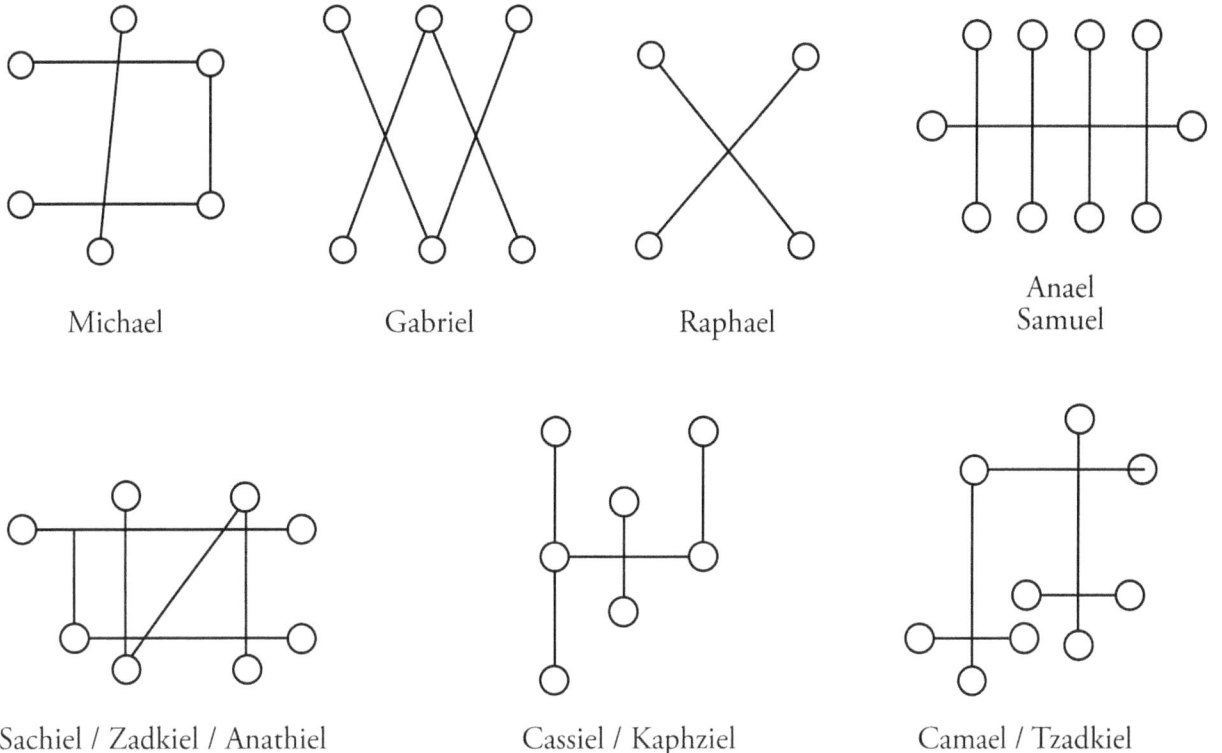

Celestial Sigils of the Archangels

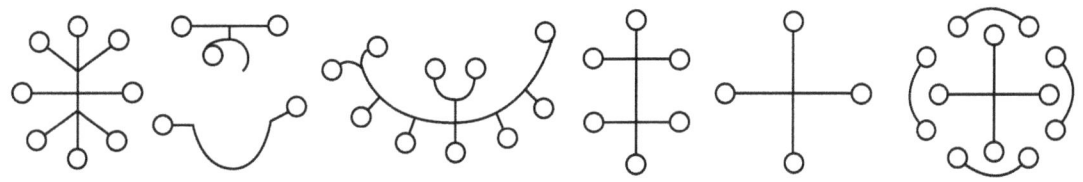

Protective Spell Written in Celestial Charakteres from Coptic Text

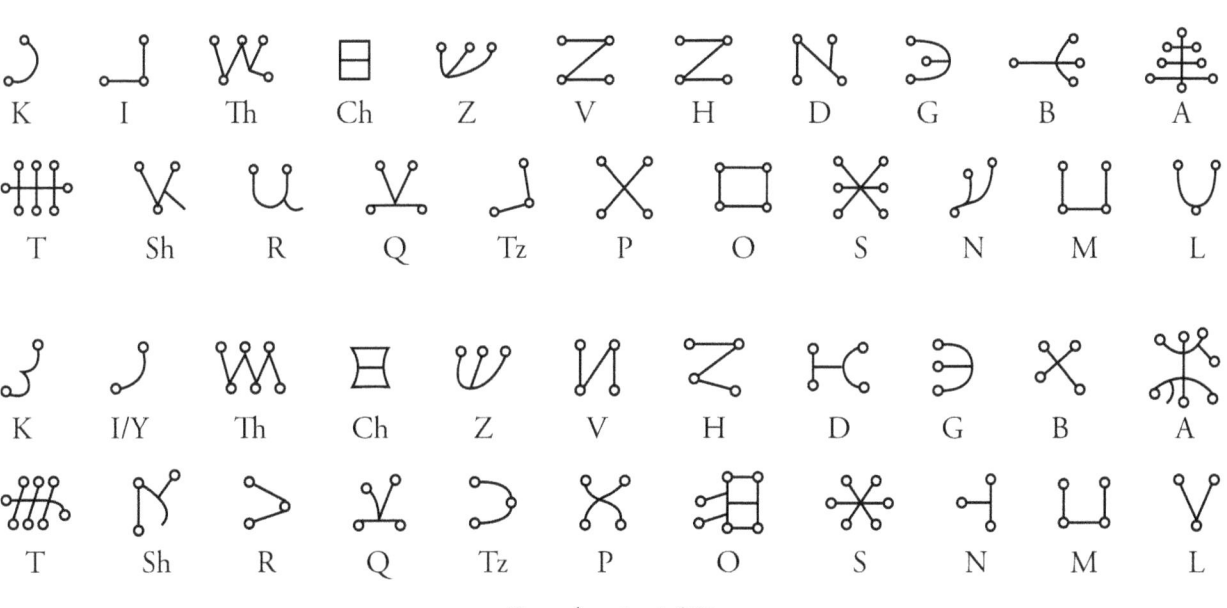

Bartolozzi - 1675

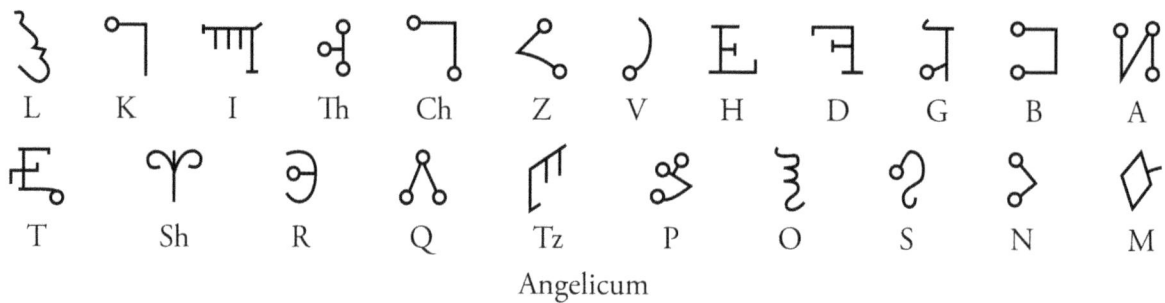
Angelicum

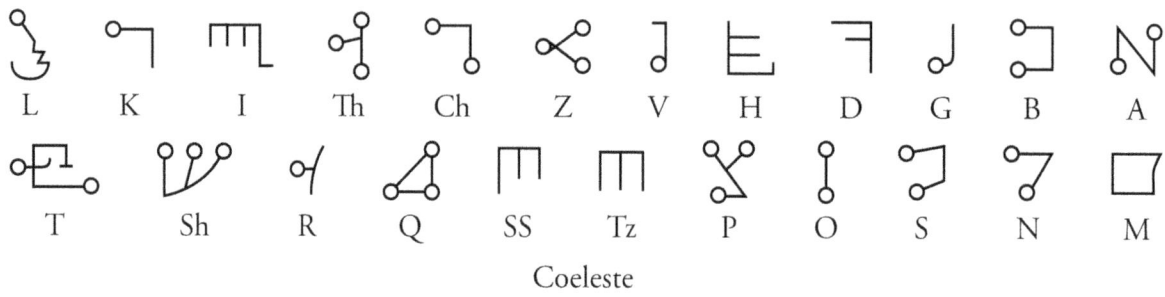
Coeleste

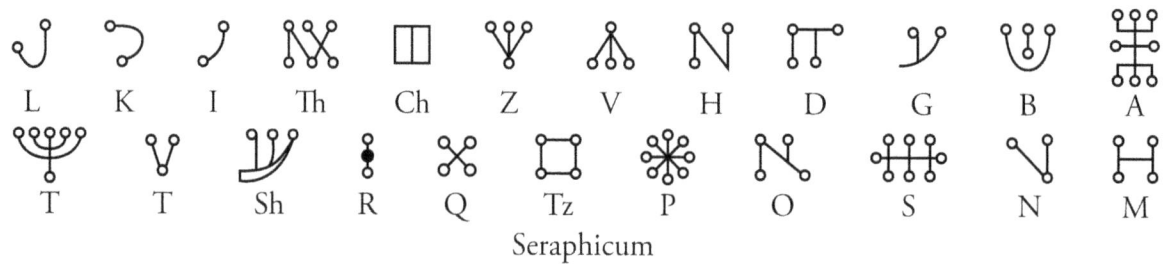
Seraphicum

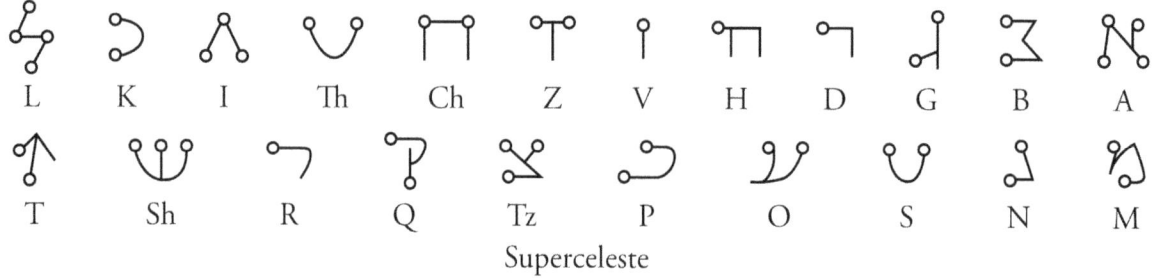
Superceleste

James Bonaventure Hepburn - Virga Aurea 1616

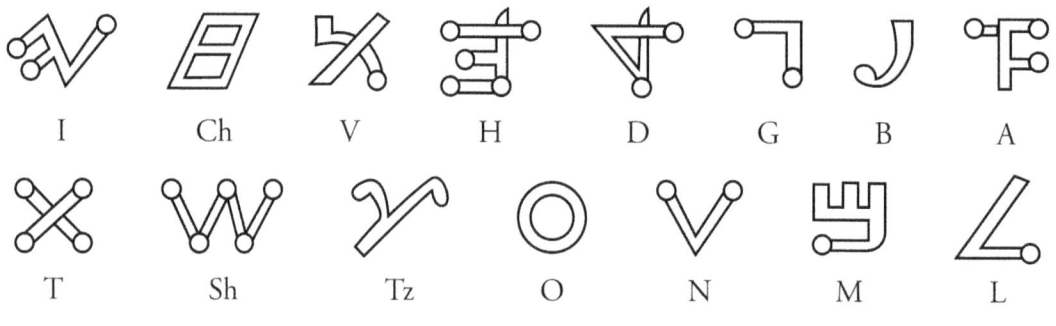
Samaritan Celestial Script

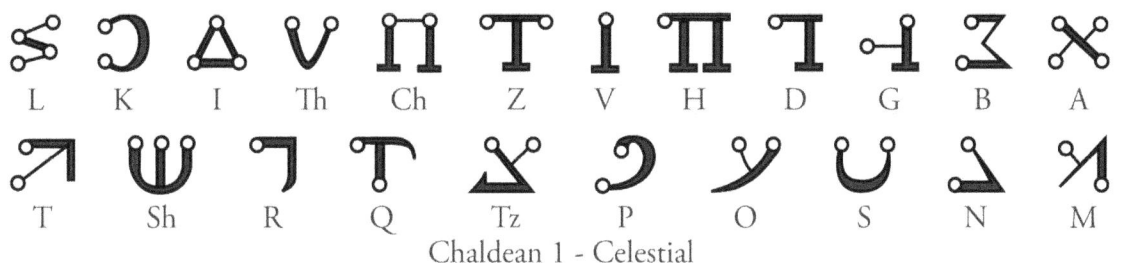
Chaldean 1 - Celestial

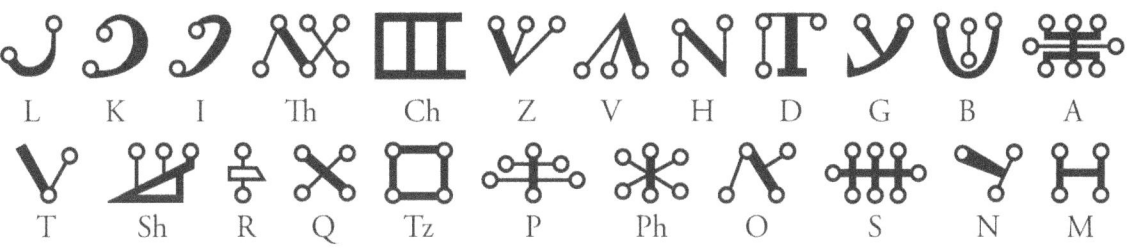
Chaldean 9 - Malachim (Mose's Tables of Law)

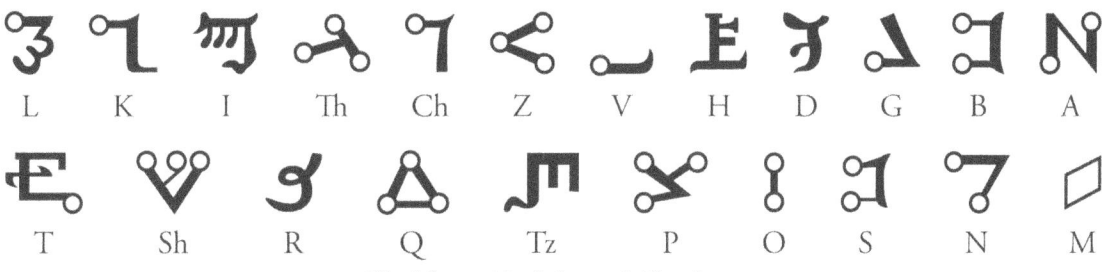
Chaldean 10 - Moses / Abraham

Edmutd Fry's Pantographia, 1788

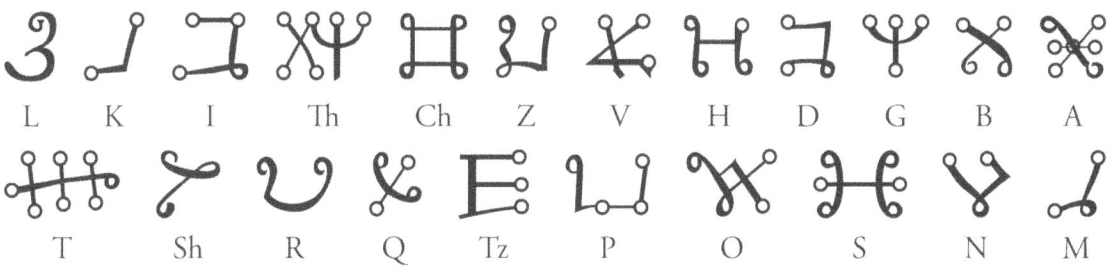
Chaldean - Anton De Pantis - 16th century

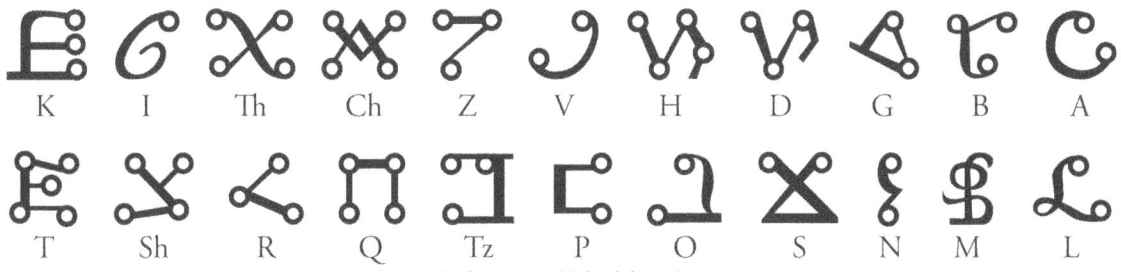
Solomon (Chaldean)

Chaldean style Celestial scripts

Enochian Scripts

During the 16th century, it became fashionable to collect ancient alphabets and scripts and attribute them to the Hebrew Patriarchs. As a result, the Enochian script style was conceived. Its principal form is a cipher for Hebrew written using calligraphic variants of the Assyrian/Ashurit script style known as Square Hebrew.

The first script in the Assyrian style was published in the 1530 treatise called the 'Voarcrino Umia' by Pantheo. It is an alphabet called Voarchadumia, attributed to Enoch. It is calculated that Pantheo formed the Voarchadumia by merging Agrippa's three Celestial scripts (Celestial, Passing the River and Writing of the Magi scripts) together in a Hebrew/Greek mix in the Assyrian calligraphic style.

The Voarchadumia script was reproduced in Edward Fry's 1778 Pantographia, and catagorized as Chaldean; an alternative name for the Assyrian script style. 'Enochaeum', published by James Bonaventure Hepburn in his Virga Aurea in 1616, is a Torahanic variation of the Square Hebrew script.

These Enochian scripts have little if anything in common with the Enochian script of Elizabethan magician's, Dr. John Dee and Sir Edward Kelly, except that they all claim to be attributed to the Patriarch Enoch in some way. Although Dee and Kelly's script bears similarities to Pantheo's in its stroke structure and stylistics, none of the actual glyphs match.

Dee and Kelly claim they were given their Enochian letter forms by the means of scrying. Scrying is a technique used to tell the future and involves gazing into a reflective surface to receive messages.

When Kelly could not aptly imitate the characters or letters as they were shown, they appeared on his paper in a light yellow colour, which he drew in black and the yellow disappeared, leaving the black letter.

Dee and Kelly's Enochian script style is considered to be a European hybrid, derived from the calligraphic mixing of Coptic uncial forms and the Fidal script of Ethiopian Christians, a popular mystic style of the time. Aleister Crowley also produced a variant for the Golden Dawn.

In the late 20th century, fantasy author, Terry Pratchett, produced a version arranged into Aetir's or families, used as a plot device in his stories.

Voarchadumia - Pantheo - 1530

Chaldean 4 / Voarchadumia - Edmurd Fry's Pantographia - 1788

Torahamic Hebrew - James Bonaventura Hepburn's Virga Aurea - 1616

Dee - 1583

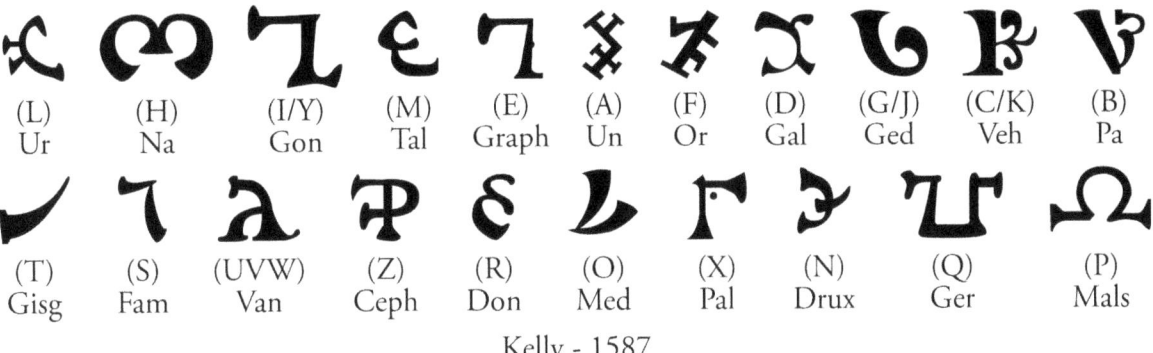

Kelly - 1587

Dee and Kelly's Enochian script and letter order written right to left

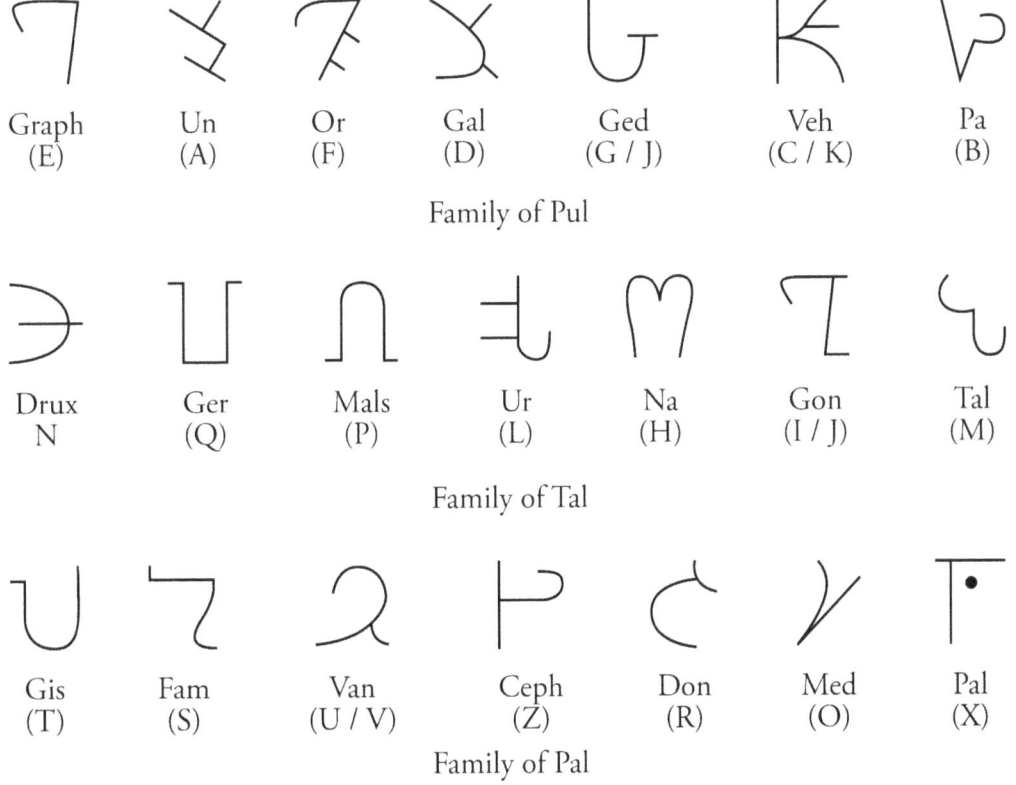

Family of Pul

Family of Tal

Family of Pal

Enochian Cursive Script and Families - Terry Pratchit

Occult Scripts

An enormous number of occult scripts have been recorded in the Western occult tradition, very many of them being of a somewhat dubious value, but a few of them used in occult literature or in various art forms have an occult heritage.

Some of these scripts are reinterpreted versions of genuine historical alphabets that have been collated from occult texts and a great many more are derived from cabalistic sources.

They were created by various adepts to express their mystical knowledge, employed as codes and ciphers for communicating with Angels or hiding esoteric knowledge, used as ciphers for Hebrew and Greek, to write the names of God and Angels on seals, pentacles and talismans. They were reproduced in a number of 15th, 16th and 17th century grimoires and polygraphia's.

The most renowned of these scripts were documented by Cornelius Agrippa in his Books of Occult Philosophy and the same scripts are found in a Table of the Mystical Alphabets published in the Key of Solomon.

The invention of the Celestial script is attributed to Agrippa. The similar-looking 'Malachim', meaning 'angel', 'messenger' or 'regal', is the Celestial script style used to write the Tables of Law given to Moses. As its name suggests, Malachim was believed to be used in Angelic writings and all communication between heavenly beings and man. Its origins are considered a mystery.

In 1523, Abraham De Balmes published a text titled, 'The Flock of Abraham'. It contained an alphabet called Katv ever ha-nahar or Script Beyond the River. It was picked up by magic enthusiasts including Agrippa who republished, it as 'Scriptura Transitus Fluvi' or 'Passing the River script'.

The name may refer to the passage of the Jewish people across the River Euphrates when they returned from Babylon to rebuild the temple at Jerusalem. Through the centuries, it has been popular with secret societies and is still used by today's high-degree Freemasons, albeit in a limited way. It is commonly used in talismanic inscriptions.

The Writing of the Magi is said to have been invented by a 16th century alchemist called Theophrastus Baubastis von Hohenhiem, better known as Paracelsus. It was used by its inventor to engrave the names of Angelic beings on talismans for treating illness and protection.

The Theban alphabet is first mentioned by Johannes Trithemius in his 16th century Polygraphia and by Agrippa, a student of Trithemius. It has one-to-one correspondences with the letters of the Latin alphabet, except for J and V. It is possible that it began life as a Latin cipher used by early 10th century alchemists to disguise the meaning of a text and give it a mystical quality.

The script is also known as the Runes of Honourus, after its reputed inventor, Honorius of Thebes; and the Witches Alphabet after it was used by Gerald Gardner, founder of the Wiccan religion, to write witches' spells, inscriptions on knives and swords, the Book of Shadow and other texts.

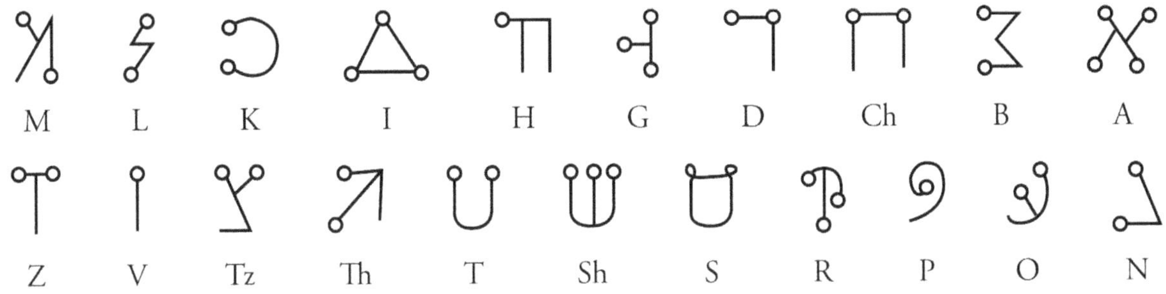

Celestial

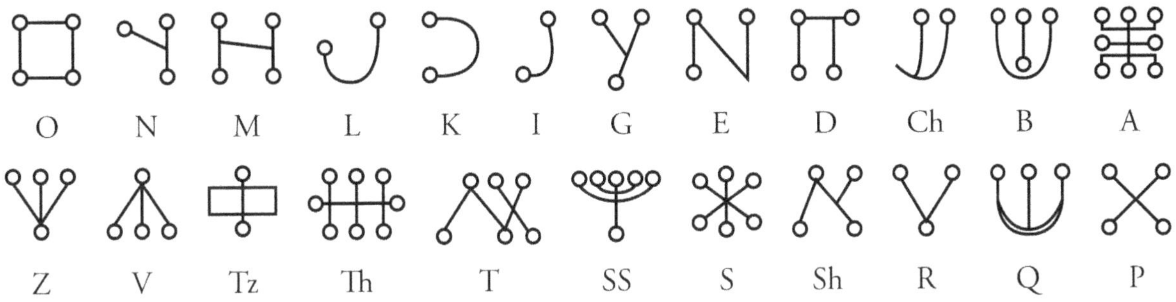

Malachim

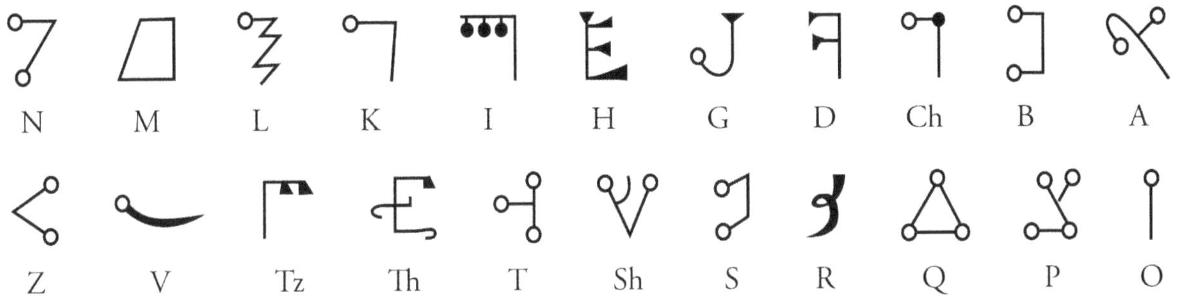

Transitus Fluvi / Passing the River Script

Celsestial cipher scripts for Writing Hebrew

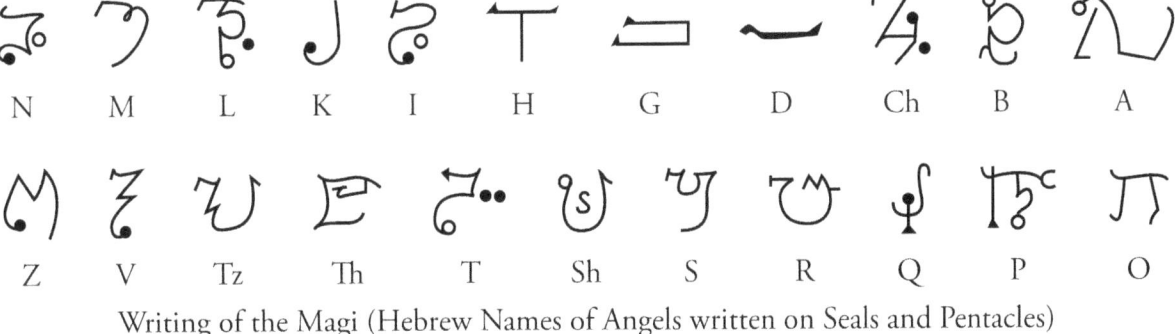

Writing of the Magi (Hebrew Names of Angels written on Seals and Pentacles)

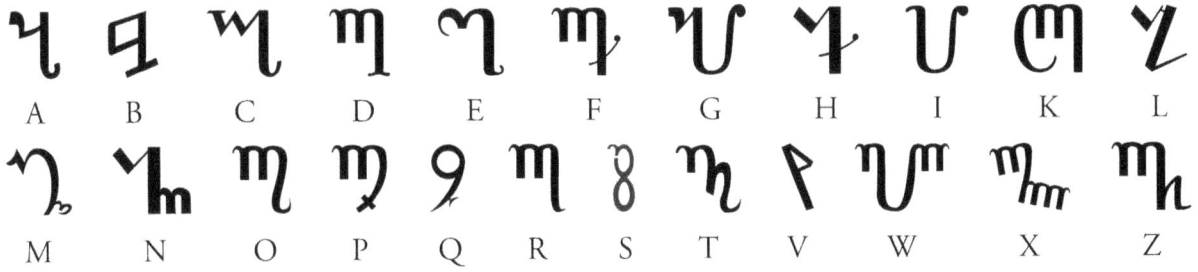

Theban / Runes of Honourius / Witches' Alphabet - Latin

Cipher scripts for Hebrew and Latin - H C Agrippa

Hermetic Scripts

Hermetic is a term used to describe individuals and societies who follow the teachings of the Thrice Great Hermes or Hermes Trismegistus, the founder of alchemy. Generally, hermetic scripts are those ciphers developed by individuals and secret societies to hide their findings or experiments, or their esoteric wisdom and knowledge from the uninitiated.

They often employ astrological, alchemical and unique signs to create ciphers for the Hebrew, Greek, Latin and English languages. Many have unique numerological systems for their secret encoding.

Among the most common are those made up of astrological and alchemical symbols, with considerable overlapping of boundaries between the two, some scripts combining both. The general idea being that sigils normally used to denote planets, zodiac constellations, alchemical substances and processes are substituted for the letters of the alphabet. There are many versions of these signs with many adepts producing their own individual variants.

Astrological signs are graphic forms of the occult interpretations of the constellations of the zodiac. The planetary symbols are based on their association with particular metals, colours, stones, herbs, flowers, trees, fruit, perfumes and animals, and are not as well-known as those of the zodiac.

The alchemical group includes by far the greatest number of symbols, mainly because, for almost two thousand years, there has been a tradition of listing sigils and their names and many lists have survived.

At the beginning of the 17th century, following the dawn of the Age of Enlightenment, the influence of magic on the European intellect faded and the transmission of Western occult knowledge was continued by secret societies like the Rosicrucians, Illuminati and Freemasons into the modern era, when they were incorporated into the teachings of the Hermetic Order of the Golden Dawn and others.

The Templar-influenced Rosicrucians were an esoteric order that arose in early 17th century Europe. A secret brotherhood of alchemists and sages whose aim was to transform the arts and sciences, and the religious, political and intellectual landscape of Europe. The Rosicrucian cipher known as The Sovereign Prince was reproduced by Helena Blavatsky in 1877.

The Illuminati were a secret society within a secret society, founded by Adam Weishaupt in Bavaria in 1776, from an existing Masonic order. All its members had secret names and they used a calendar based on the ancient Persian system. Their alphabet contains three forms of encoding which were published in A History of Secret Societies by Akron Daraud. There are two symbol ciphers and a unique number cipher.

The number cipher begins with A=12, B=11, and so on, until M=1. Then N=13, O=15 and so on, until Z=24. The letters I and J, and U and V, are represented by the same number. This unique number cipher plays an important role in Illuminati numerology which stresses the numbers 3, 7, 9, 11, 13, 33, 39 in their formulae.

In the English alphabet, the letter M is the 13th letter and denotes the middle of the letter sequence. The letter M derives from the Semitic word 'mem' meaning 'water'. The Illuminati translate the word 'water' as meaning 'Elixir of Life'.

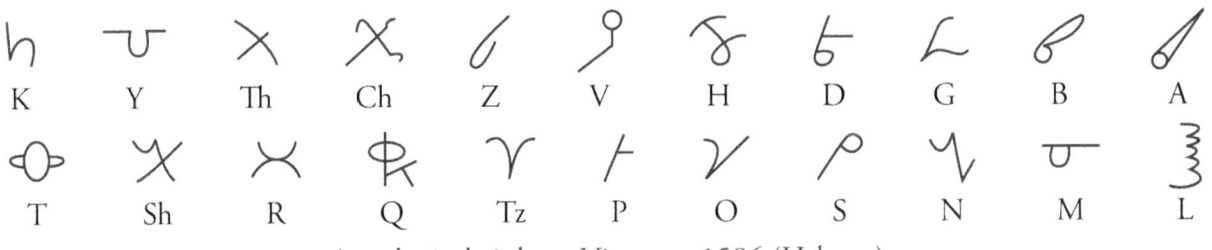

Astrological cipher - Vignere - 1586 (Hebrew)

Alchemical cipher - Vignere - 1586

Spanish Inquisiton cipher - Vignere - 1586

Rosicruscian cipher / 'The Sovereign Prince' - Blavatsky - 1877

Fred Gettings - Dictionary of Occult, Alchemical and Hermetic Sigils

Illuminati ciphers - 17th century

Aleister Crowley's Scripts

Born Edward Crowley in 1875, Aleister Crowley was an infamous 20th century British occultist, the self-styled Great Beast, who changed his name to Aleister following a life-changing vision that showed him the way to his spiritual vocation.

He founded the religion of Thelema, identifying himself as the prophet entrusted with guiding humanity into the Aeon of Horus in the early 20th century. He died in 1947.

In late 19th century Britain, there was a revival of interest in Hermetic occultism and Crowley was a product of that revival. Just like Helena Blavatsky and the Theosophists, Crowley was heavily influenced by Indian and Chinese philosophy and imagery but the magic practices of the Hermetic Order of the Golden Dawn included ancient Egyptian and Greek rites and imagery which was more appealing to Crowley. Crowley went on to be become the most influential figure that came to prominence on the early 20th century occult scene.

After becoming involved with secretive groups like the Golden Dawn, Aurum Solis and Ordo Templis Orientalis, Crowley gradually evolved a full set of beliefs he called Thelema, which drew on Oriental, Egyptian and an assortment of occult practices such as astrology, divination, numerology, inner alchemy and necromancy.

As an esoteric and occult society of spiritual thought, Thelema (meaning 'to will, wish, wait or purpose') is a religious philosophy based on the Book of the Law written by Crowley and has parallels with Eastern religions, especially Buddhism.

According to Crowley, the Law of Thelema or the Law of Will written in 1904, was dictated to him whilst he was in Egypt by an ancient Egyptian spirit called Aiwass. It laid out the key principle of life as Crowley saw it; the pursuit of each individual's will, unconstrained by popular opinion, law or conventional ethics. This concerned his major and much misinterpreted statement of "Do what thy will, shall be the whole of the Law". He interpreted it as meaning "follow the true path to find one's free will".

Thelemic theology utilizes the divinities of various cultures and religions as personifications of specific divine, archetypical and cosmic forces. Its doctrine holds that all diverse religions of humanity are grounded in universal truths.

It follows traditional Hermeticism, in which each person has a soul or light-body wrapped in layers or sheaths surrounding the physical body, and each individual has a Guardian Angel which is both the higher self and a separate sentient being.

Thelema has a pantheon of gods including adaptations of ancient Egyptian gods and Crowley also associated Thelemic spiritual practices with concepts rooted in Western and Eastern occultism, integrating practices from hermeticism, cabala and yoga.

Crowley's thought in general, inspired the rise of modern Neopaganism and some variations of Satanism. His influence on Neopagan movements is derived from his Magnum Opus, Magic in Theory and Practice, published in 1929. His definition of magic can be found in the modern witchcraft movement.

He became a significant influence upon the founders of a variety of new religious movements, and occultists including Gerald Gardner, the founder of Wicca, and Austin Osman Spare, whose sigilization technique became the cornerstone of Chaos Magick.

Many of Crowley's ideas found their way into expressions of the Counter Culture of the 1960s and 70s, and the so-called Dawn of the Age of Aquarius through Rock and Roll music, when his ideas influenced the thoughts of certain Satanists including Anton Le Vey, founder of the Church of Satan.

Crowley published the ciphers in his book, 'The Vision and the Voice', a visionary journey through the realms or "aethyrs" inhabited by the Enochian Angels. The Alphabet of Arrows is a cipher for the Enochian alphabet. It is related to the Dagger script, a cipher using the Latin alphabet as a base. Their inner forms are the same, their outer forms differ; one using a bow and arrow, the other a dagger. His Alphabet of Angels is a unique styling of the Aiq Bkr cipher symbols. He also produced a more refined form of Dee and Kelly's Enochian script.

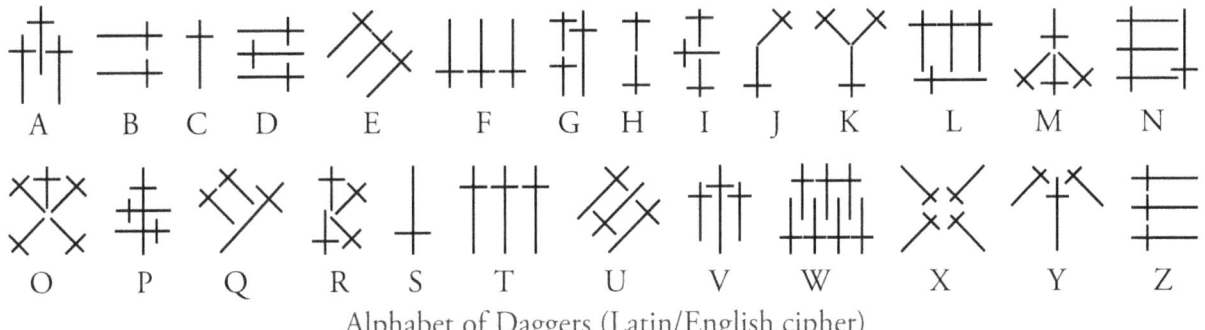

Alphabet of Daggers (Latin/English cipher)

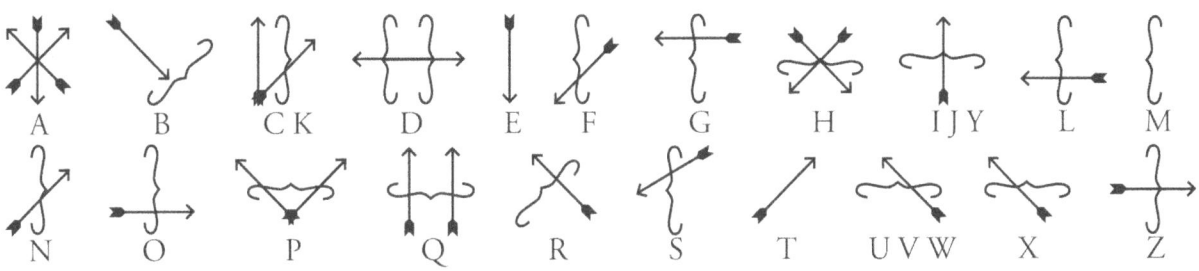

Alphabet of Angels (Aiq Bkr cipher)

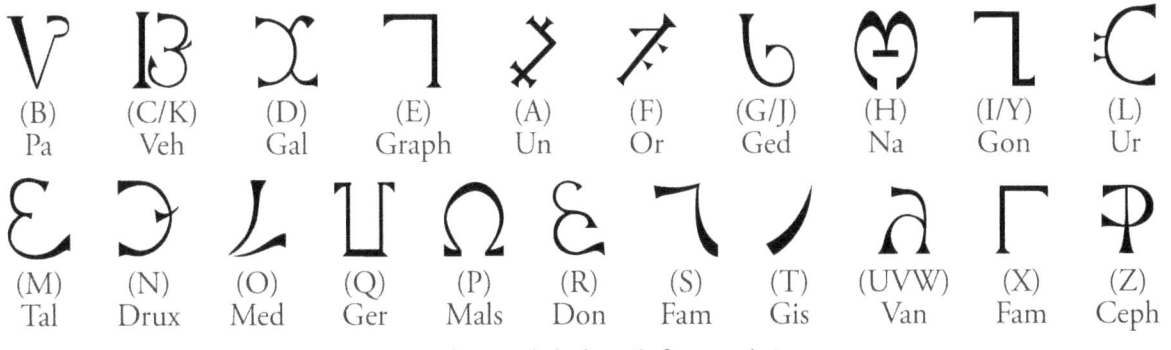

Alphabet of Arrows (Enochian cipher)

(B)	(C/K)	(D)	(E)	(A)	(F)	(G/J)	(H)	(I/Y)	(L)
Pa	Veh	Gal	Graph	Un	Or	Ged	Na	Gon	Ur

(M)	(N)	(O)	(Q)	(P)	(R)	(S)	(T)	(UVW)	(X)	(Z)
Tal	Drux	Med	Ger	Mals	Don	Fam	Gis	Van	Fam	Ceph

Enochian Alphabet (left to right)

British Neopagan Scripts

Also called modern and contemporary paganism to distinguish itself from traditional paganism, Neopaganism covers a widely varied set of spiritual practices adopted from pre-Christian European religions like Heathenism, witchcraft, shamanism and modern anti-Christian religions such as Satanism.

Identical to European Neopaganism, British Neopaganism begins in the 18th century with the Age of Enlightenment, whose logic inspired a fading of belief in witchcraft, leading to the publication of the 1760 Witchcraft Act in England that no longer sought the death penalty for witchcraft. In the same century, the Romantic movement saw the beginning of a renewed interest in Norse and Celtic art, literature and religion.

This continued throughout the 19th century as paganism came to the attention of British mystics through various international events and cultural developments, including fresh archeological discoveries in Egypt, and a growing interest in Egyptian history, the formation of the Folklore Society in 1878 and the late Victorian Celtic renaissance that inspired authors, artists, philosophers, scientists and lay people to increasingly turn to Celtic, Norse, Egyptian, Greco-Roman and other forms of paganism for inspiration and values that were not driven by contemporary industrialism, materialism and consumerism.

By the early 20th century, there were established Heathen brotherhoods, Druid groves and witches' covens in Britain. In 1945, Robert Graves published his influential book, The White Goddess, in which Celtic mythologies are reconstructed. The repeal of the Witchcraft Act in 1951 allowed Gerald Gardner to publish Witchcraft Today in 1954, laying the foundation stone of Wicca.

This situation gave rise not only to Wicca but to Neo-Druidism, goddess-worship, Earth religions, New Age movements, Neoshamanism, Luciferianism and Satanism, all predominantly British in origin.

The Neopagan movement in Britain is primarily represented by Wicca and witchcraft religions, followed by Druidry, then Heathenism plus various Satanic and New Age groups. These groups remained underground until popularized during the Counter Culture revolution of the 1960s and 70s, as Druids appeared with John Lennon and Stonehenge became a focus for New Age devotees.

At the same time, Heathens reintroduced the Norse runes to Europe, North America and Australia, following their abandonment after the Second World War, due to their association with the Aryanism of the German Nazi party.

British Neopagan scripts fall into two categories; those that have been revived from the past and those new scripts based on pagan symbolism with no occult or literary history.

Out of these British scripts, the most authentic are the Irish, Biobel Loath script and the Barddas or Bardic runes, used to write the Welsh Druidic text called the Barddas; both revived by 19th century Celtic Romantics.

New scripts are derived from Scottish Neopaganism. Pecta Wita is the modern revival name for Scottish or ancient Pictish paganism. The Pecti Wita rune script has no antiquity and is used mainly for fortune-telling.

The Pictish swirl script is said to be part of the ancient Pictish writing system, although it is thought that the ancient Picts employed no alphabetic writing system. As a cipher for the English alphabet, it is inspired by the spiral patterns found on ancient Pictish stonework and is used for spell-casting.

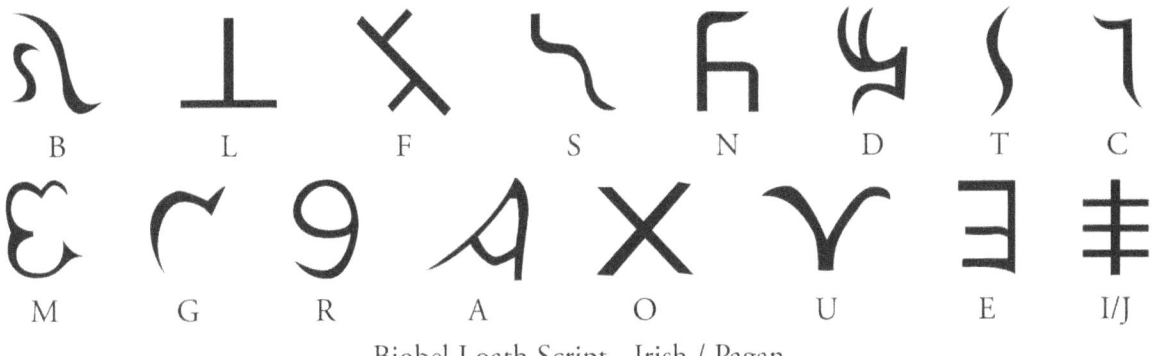
Biobel Loath Script - Irish / Pagan

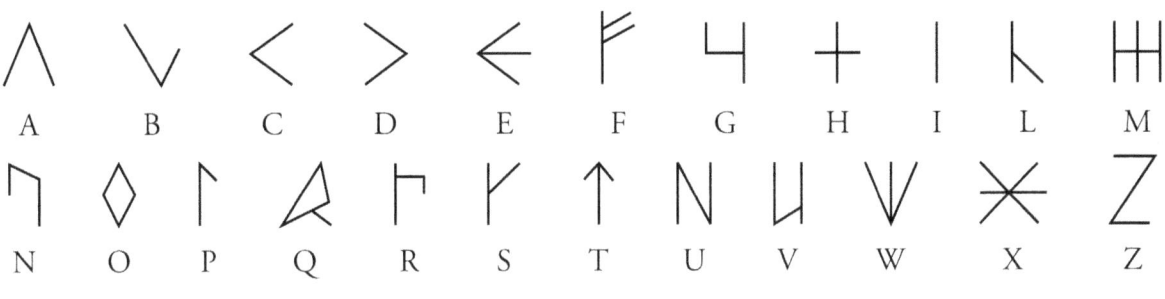
Bardic or Barddas Runes - Welsh / Pagan

Pecti Wita Runes - Scottish / Neopagan

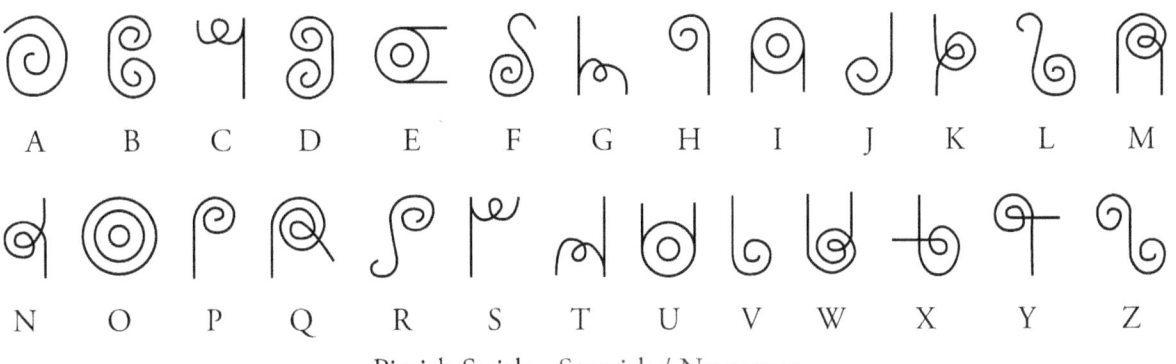
Pictish Swirls - Scottish / Neopagan

Aiq Bkr Cipher

In Jewish mysticism, the Aiq Bkr is a substitution or Temurah cipher for the 22 letters of the Hebrew alphabet. Aiq Bkr or 'the cabala of nine chambers', is a magic square with a grid of nine cells. The letters of the Hebrew alphabet are written left to right across the grid, and down and across the 3 x 3 grid, with each of the nine chambers containing three letters. In Hebrew, this includes the final forms of K, M, N, P, Q, to bring the number of letters equal to the number of squares in the grid.

When the cipher is written, the script looks like a simple graphic design. The letters are formed from angled lines and dots that indicate the position of the letter in the magic square, enabling the script to be deciphered. For example, the first letter of the cell is denoted by an angled line only. The second letter uses the same angled sign as the first but includes a single dot. The third letter in the cell has two dots placed above the same angled sign.

To create a sigil, first encode the Hebrew name using the Aiq Bkr cipher, then compress it before rearranging the elements to compose a sigil.

The occult cipher for the English alphabet is based on the cabalistic Aiq Bkr cipher for Hebrew. It is the original 'box cipher' for the alphabet and was one of several similar systems described by Agrippa and adapted by the Rosicrucians and the Freemasons.

As with Hebrew, the English letters of the alphabet are arranged in a 3 x 3 grid. Each square of the grid contains three letters, written across and down, from left to right, the ampersand is used to equal the number of letters in the Aiq Bkr sequence.

The cipher works by taking the English spelling of the name to be ciphered and locating each letter on the grid. The letter is denoted by its position within the cell and the position of the cell within the grid. When the cipher is written, the script looks like a simple graphic design.

Agrippa also described how the Aiq Bkr characters can be combined to form Olympian Sigils to encode the names of the celestial spirits called the Olympian Angels. Although Agrippa showed several such systems, the method shown is based on one provided by Francis Barrett in The Magus.

First, encode the name or word using the Aiq Bkr cipher and condense its form. Next, replace the dots with vertical lines topped by triangles to further encode the sigil. To encode it even further, draw a connecting line joining those letters that stand on the same line in the cipher.

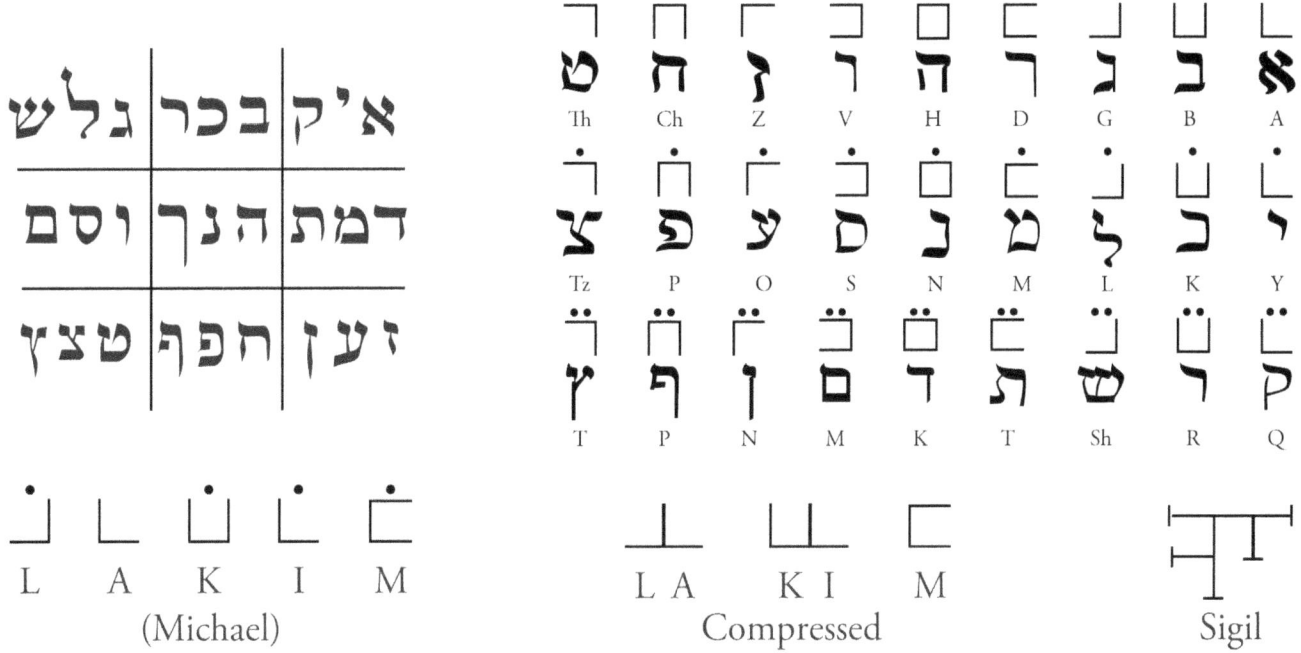

Aiq Bkr / Nine Chambers Cipher - H C Agrippa

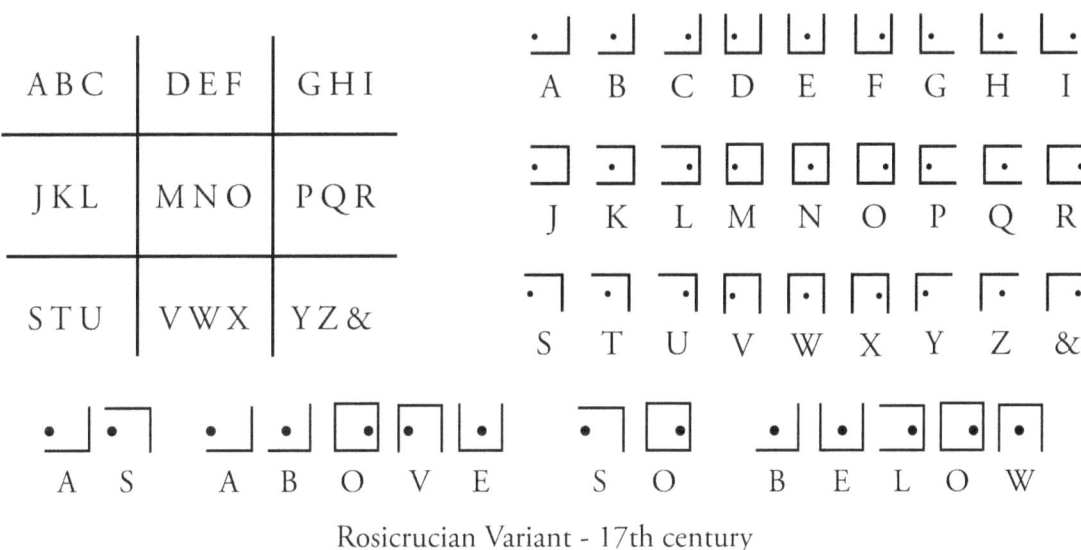

Rosicrucian Variant - 17th century

Olympic Sigil - Michael

Masonic Ciphers

On the orders of Emperor Theodorus in 339 CE, early Christians burnt libraries and smashed the relics of the pagan gods, bringing an end to the mystery cults of the ancient world, Isis and Osiris, Mithras, Serapis, Demeter, Apollo, Dionysus and Mani. At this time, cult members disappeared and did not resurface again until the 17th century with the publication of the Rosicrucian manifesto and the 18th century Masonic rituals.

Those magic alphabets that are better called magic ciphers are, in the main, invented by closed societies such as the Freemasons. They use them to keep their knowledge a secret, being a substitute system in which the signs change but they retain the underlying grammatical construction of an alphabet. Our normal alphabet is a cipher replete with secrets that go way beyond being more than visual symbols of sound.

There are various devices used to create magic ciphers derived from the idea of the Jewish Aiq Bkr magic square system. The Rosicrucians adapted the English alphabet to the Aiq Bkr square. The Masonic pigpen cipher is an adaptation of the Aiq Bkr square and includes a saltire cross shape.

The Knights Templar adapted the Aiq Bkr system to their emblem, the Crusader or Maltese cross. They divided the cross into six star-forms of four cells and placed two letters in alphabetic sequence in each cell. The letters were represented by angled lines and dots as a cipher for the English alphabet. They used it as a secret code in their letters of credit.

From the 17th century onwards, the Freemasons have employed their own system called the pigpen cipher. In the pigpen system, the letters of the alphabet are placed in twos in a 3 x 3 grid and an X shape or pigpen. When written, the letters are ciphered in the same manner as Aiq Bkr. The Masons used this script in their architecture, enabling secret meanings and messages to be publicly displayed in their churches, lodges and temples.

The Royal Arch is possibly the best known of the Masonic ciphers. Its name refers to one of the degrees within Freemasonry. It is based on the pigpen grid systems of two letters in each cell of a 3 x 3 grid. The remaining letters are placed in twos in the four segments of an X-shaped figure. A variant of the Royal Arch cipher is the Nug Soth cipher.

The Blue Lodge cipher is another Masonic cipher. It uses the same pigpen cipher technique. Except for the letters that spell the word (?) Mason that occupy the first five positions on the grid, the remaining 22 letters follow in alphabetic sequence.

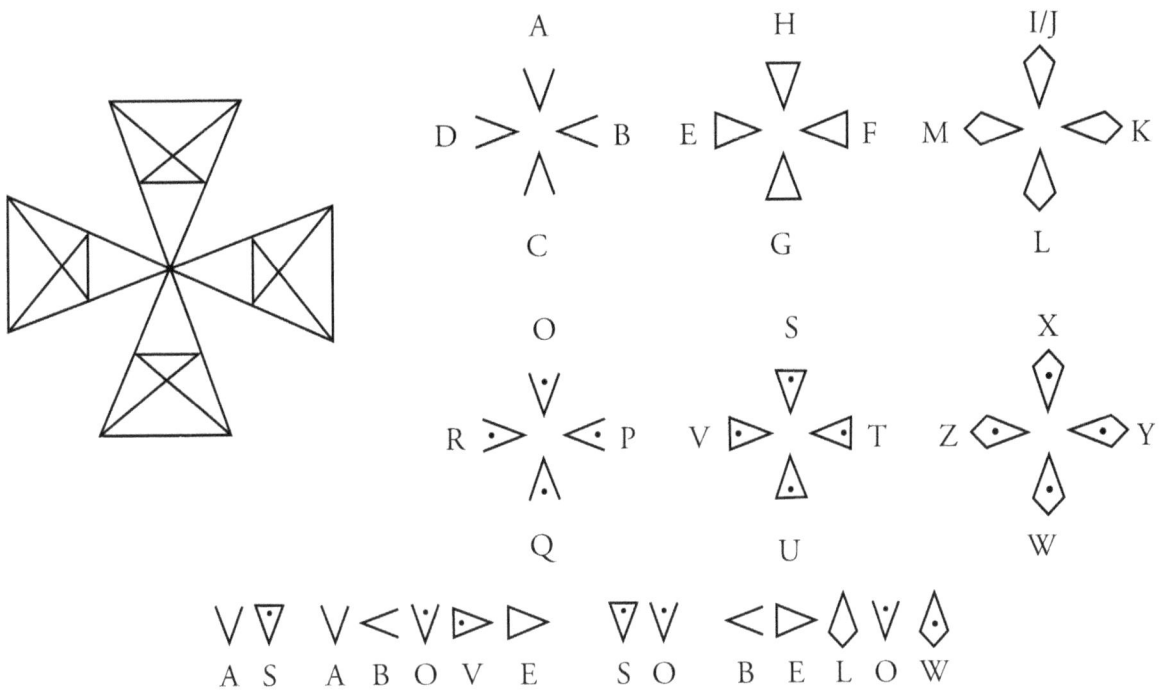

Knights Templar Cipher - 12th century

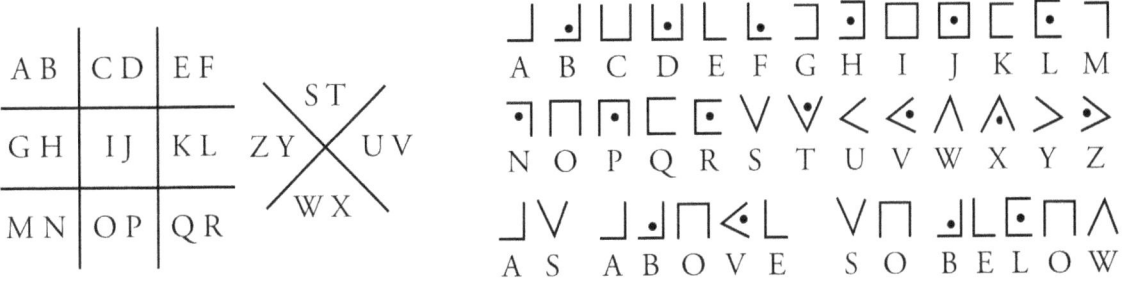

Royal Arch Cipher of the Freemasons

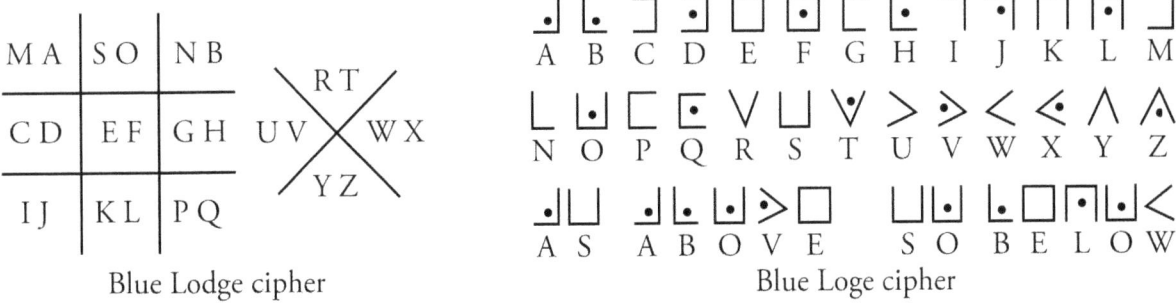

Blue Lodge cipher   Blue Loge cipher

Masonic 'pig pen' ciphers - 17/18th century

Sigil Ciphers

Various methods of encoding the letters of the alphabet have been developed over the millennia. The majority of these use the letters of the alphabet in either a sequential or re-ordered form associated with the numerology linked with kamea or magic squares.

Some kamea employ alpha-numerology to find the occult signature of the name of an entity, angel, demon or other spirit. This classic method stems from the practice of isosephy, invented by the Greek scholar, Pythagoras, circa 600 BCE, in which each letter of the alphabet is assigned to the numbers 1–9, giving the letters of a word a 'numerical order' which can be traced out on a 3 x 3 magic square.

These spirit signatures or sigils are created by converting the name of a spirit to a numerical form using an alpha-numeric code and number square. The location of the numbers within the square are connected in sequence by a line to form an abstract figure that becomes the spirit's sigil or occult signature. The most potent of these sigils are the ones that can be drawn in a single line without taking the pen off the paper.

The style of the sigil is created by drawing an open circle round the first number, then a line is drawn to pass through each number in sequence without the pen leaving the paper and it is finished with a terminal stroke or closed circle on the last number. The circle and the terminal line denote the beginning and ending of a name or word. A loop is used to denote double letters – EE, OO, TT, etc., and a double bump denotes the use of two letters in the same square. Once devised, the sigil may be mirrored, rotated, perfected and artistically embellished.

Various forms of letter ciphers are used to create spirit sigils. In the Middle Ages and Renaissance, magicians published spirit sigils in magical training books called grimoires such as the Key of Solomon. Sigils are central to the Ceremonial magic of necromancy, 'communication with the dead'; the occult practice the modern mind most associates with black magic

In the early 20th century, the Hermetic order of the Golden Dawn created the Rosy Cross Cipher, based on the Double Star of the Sepher Yetzirah, providing a simpler method of constructing sigils for spirits with Hebrew names. Names in any other language will not work with this cipher. The Golden Dawn Enochian Rose Cipher can be used to create Enochian sigils. Both use the same sigil creation rules as with kamea.

Other letter ciphers include a version of Agrippa's construction of the 5 x 5 kamea and the QWERTY keyboard letter order.

The Witches' Wheel is a cipher for names or words spelt in English. Witches sigils may be looped around the letters and can be artistically embellished to increase its magical effect.

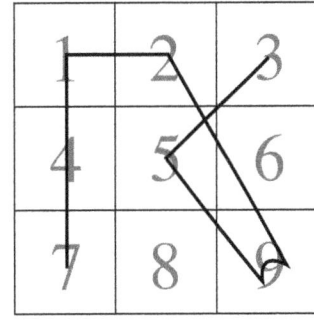
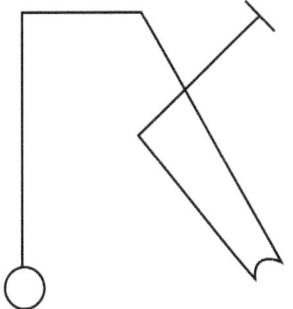

Letter / Number Values   3 x 3 Magic Square   Sigil of Gabriel
Spirit Sigil

Hebrew   Hebrew. Raphael - correct   Hebrew/Latin. Raphael - incorrect

Golden Dawn Rosy Cross Cipher (Double Star of the Sefer Yetzirah)

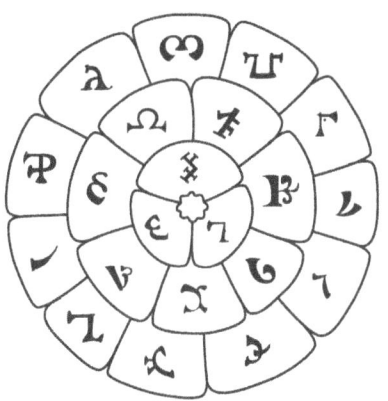
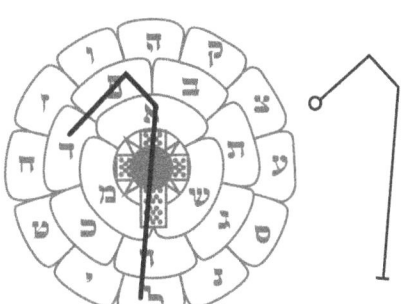
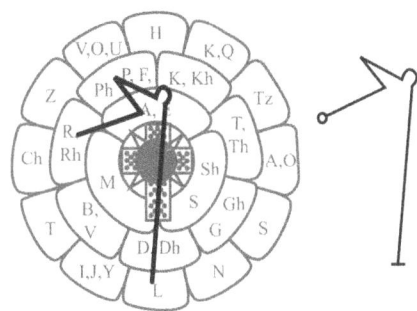

Rosy Cross - Enochian   Agrippa's 5 x 5 Kamea   QWERTY keyboard

Letter Cipher Squares

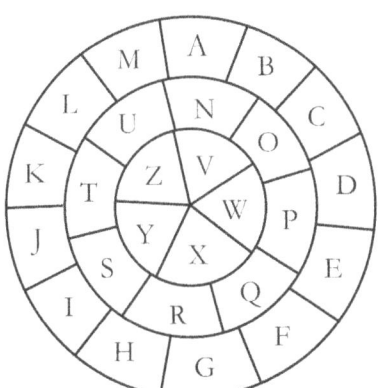
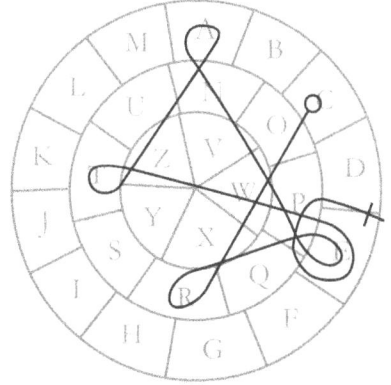

Witches Wheel / English   'Create' - looped sigil   'Creation' - Artistic embellishment refined / rotated / mirrored

Witches' Wheel - 'Create' sigil

Further Reading

The Story of Writing
Andrew Robinson – Thames & Hudson

The Blackwell Encyclopaedia of Writing Systems
Florian Coulmas – Blackwell Publishing

The White Goddess
Robert Graves – Faber & Faber

The Secret Science of Numerology
Shirley Blackwell Lawrence – New Page Books

The Greek Cabala
Kieran Barry – Weiser

Book of Occult Philosophy
Cornelius Agrippa

777 and other Cabalistic Writings
Aleister Crowley – Weiser

The Vision and the Voice
Aleister Crowley

Rune Power
Kenneath Meadows – Rider

The Secret of the Runes
Guido Von List

The Secret King, Karl Maria Wiligut, Himmler's Lord of the Runes
Stephene Flowers – Dominion / Rine Raven

The Book of Runes
Robert Blum – Michael Joseph

Virga Aurea
James Bonaventura Hepburn

Pantographia
Edmund Fry

Dictionary of Occult, Alchemical and Hermetic Sigils
Fred Gettings

www.ingramcontent.com/pod-product-compliance
Ingram Content Group UK Ltd.
Pitfield, Milton Keynes, MK11 3LW, UK
UKHW050636280925
463391UK00013B/83